You Can't Climb A Tree In A Dress

MAUREEN BROOKS SLATER

You Can't Climb A Tree In A Dress
Copyright © 2019 by Maureen Brooks Slater

All rights reserved. No part of this publication may be reproduced, distributed, or transmitted in any form or by any means, including photocopying, recording, or other electronic or mechanical methods, without the prior written permission of the author, except in the case of brief quotations embodied in critical reviews and certain other non-commercial uses permitted by copyright law.

Tellwell Talent
www.tellwell.ca

ISBN
978-0-2288-1122-0 (Paperback)

To Rick

You presented me with a blank journal and encouraged me to get writing. You loved hearing these extraordinary stories over the years and somehow made me believe I needed to write this short book of childhood memories.
Thank you for loving me, supporting me,
and for always being my anchor.
I love and appreciate you so much.

Acknowledgments

I dedicate this book to my late parents, **Henry** and **Marjorie Brooks**. To my father who understood me completely, and my mother, who was unwavering in her love but never entirely sure what to make of her youngest child. My parents would have loved seeing these stories in print.

This book is for my sisters, **Eileen** and **Rosalie**. We share so many fond childhood memories. The stories I have written about are the ones you seem to most enjoy recalling. We were close as children and are best friends as adults. I love you both very much.

It is for my son **Curtis**, who took the time to read and comment on what I had written. Thanks for your input Curt. I so enjoy our talks and appreciate hearing your perspective on things. You are a man of great wisdom, insight and patience. I love you so much and I am very proud to be your mother.

It is for my daughter **Shannon**, who was instrumental in the writing of this book. A friend of mine heard some of my childhood stories and entertained her children each night with a "Mrs. Slater" bedtime story. It wasn't long before her daughter was repeating these stories to Shannon on the school bus. Shannon was very curious about the outrageous tales her friend was sharing and wanted to know if the stories were in fact true. I assured her they were and promised to one day share all of them with her. I hope you enjoy the book Shannon, and that it was worth the wait. I love you so much and I am extremely proud of you. You are a patient, wise and loving mom to your four children, and an awesome friend to me.

It is for my son **Craig**, who worked on the cover of my book and did an incredible job. You seemed to grasp exactly what I had envisioned. You are so talented Craig. You have a kind and gentle spirit and a wonderful sense of humor. You remind me of your Grandpa Brooks in so many ways. I love you very much and I am so proud of you.

This book is for my eight precious grandchildren, **Charlie Slater Popowich, Jake William Slater, Addison April Olivia Popowich, Cole Richard Slater, Nora Rose Popowich, Noah Brooks Slater, Jonas Brooks Popowich,** and **Leo Curtis Eli Slater**. You are the light of my life. I had no idea grandkids would be so much fun. I love each of you more than you will ever know, and more than I ever thought possible. I am blessed beyond measure, and so very grateful for each one of you.

This book is for my niece **Cathie**. You walked my old neighborhood with me several years ago while I shared some of my stories. You took pictures along the way and encouraged me to write about it. It took a while, but I finally got around to it.

It is for my nephews, **Michael**, **Shane** and **Scott**. Your moms' childhood memories are interwoven with mine and they share in this story.

It is for my son-in-law **Jonathan**, and my daughter-in- laws, **Karyn** and **Mandi**. You are a much-loved part of our family story.

About the Author

I was born in Winnipeg, Manitoba on a Friday the 13th. I grew up in a middle-class neighborhood, in a cozy, three-bedroom, one-bathroom home. I didn't just march to the beat of a different drummer–I sprinted, dashed, scurried, skedaddled and zoomed! My childhood was anything but dull, and I got into a fair bit of mischief.

These are actual accounts of my childhood exploits. The adventure loving, thrill seeking little girl still lives somewhere deep inside, and wrote these stories to the best of her recollection. These stories have been told and retold by family members over the years. I have changed most names to shield the innocent. My name finds its way onto the pages and regretfully admits my guilt. I take full responsibility for every premature grey hair that turned up on my poor mother's head.

Psalm 91:11

"For He shall give His angels charge over you,
to guard you in all your ways"

My Friend Kenny

Mom was a huge fan of dresses and would have loved me to wear one every day. Dresses are okay for some things, but not suitable for the truly fun activities. I was not one for sitting around looking pretty, so play clothes worked much better for me. My favorite pastime was climbing trees. Dresses and trees do not go together... they just don't.

Towering Elms lined the boulevards of Newman street in the 50s, and I climbed every one. The taller the tree the better. I would set my sights on the highest branch and scramble up. From the top of the tree I would take a quick peek at the ground far below, and be scared to death. It sometimes felt as if my heart would pound right out of my chest. I would close my eyes, wrap my arms and legs in a death grip around the trunk, and hang on for dear life. Terrified of letting go, but not wanting to stay up in a tree for the rest of my life, I would force my eyes open, release my grasp, and inch downward. When my feet hit solid ground, I would breathe a huge sigh of relief. For reasons I can't really explain, I would then move onto the next tree and do it all over again.

Mom was not a fan of me climbing trees, and would scream in horror, "Maureen, come down from that tree!" She often said she would scour the treetops before looking on the ground when she needed to find me.

Kenny, the cute curly-haired boy who lived at the end of our street, shared my fondness for tree climbing. Together we climbed almost every tree on our block.

Kenny had three sisters, one brother, a German Shepherd dog, and a kind, soft-spoken mother. His dad was a bad-tempered sort of guy who drank beer from a brown bottle while walking around the house in his undershirt. Kenny's dad was a milkman and would sometimes park his milk truck behind their house. Kenny and I loved playing in that truck, despite the sour milk stink inside. We would sit in the well-worn, brown leather seat with our hand on the big stick shift, and turn the huge steering wheel back and forth, making believe we were delivering milk to the houses. Kenny's dad would spot us from the kitchen window and holler, "Get the heck out of the truck!" He didn't actually say heck, he used a word that would have gotten my mouth washed out with soap if I dared use it within earshot of my mom. When Kenny's dad shouted, we instantly obeyed. You did not want to risk getting a second warning from that guy.

I married at the young age of six. Kenny had a nine-year-old sister Annie, who decided Kenny and I would make a perfect couple. Annie was the wedding planner, and we were the bride and groom. Kenny was five years old and inclined to do everything his older sister asked of him. I had nothing more pressing to do at the moment, so agreed to this silly charade. Annie hurried off to the basement and returned with wedding clothes. She stuck a yellowed, musty smelling veil on my head, and pulled it down to cover my face. She yanked the faded plastic flowers out of the vase on the coffee table and placed them in my hands. An old hat and large brown sports jacket completed Kenny's outfit. We stood side by side while Annie, the respected cleric, took her place in front of us. Annie recited her version of the wedding vows while holding an official looking book... letter A of the Encyclopedia Britannica. By the power invested in a much older nine-year-old girl, we were wed. Annie said we had to kiss, but we refused saying it was gross, and skedaddled out of there.

This was the start of an exciting, adventure filled friendship. Kenny and I got into a fair amount of mischief together...

The Dogs of Newman Street

I thought Kenny was one of the luckiest kids on earth because he had a dog. I wanted a dog more than anything in the world and pestered my mom every single day, "May I have a dog? May I please have a dog? Please, please, please, may I have a dog?" Mom was not one to yield under pressure, so my endless petitions and heartfelt appeals had little effect on her. She tried to convince me we already had a pet and didn't need another. The pet she was referring to was Mickey, our little yellow canary. Mickey would puff out his throat and sing his little heart out. He would nibble on sticks of seed and flap his wings like crazy as he bathed in his birdbath. If we left his cage door open, he would fly around the kitchen and perch on the curtain rod for long periods of time. Mickey was nice enough for a bird, but I wanted a dog.

There were several dogs on Newman Street. Folks just opened their doors and let them out to roam the neighborhood all day. That was the way it worked for us kids too. We would play outside all day, and as long as we were home in time for supper, no one questioned our whereabouts.

I took a personal interest in several dogs on our street and neighborhood. I would drag them home and lock them in our yard or veranda. Giving them something to eat almost always guaranteed they would stay for a while. Most times it wasn' for too long, because my mother would hear the barking and scratching and set my captives free. When there were no dogs around our yard, or at our door begging for food, I would go to the house at the end of the street and ask if I could walk their little dog Smokey. I sometimes got the impression they thought I was a rather odd little kid for asking to walk their dog. It did not seem strange to me, and I didn't care what they thought, as long as they let me borrow their dog for a while. They would hand me Smokey's leash and send him out the door. Smokey and I would walk up one side of the street and down the other. I hoped that people passing thought Smokey was my dog.

One of my favorite dogs on the street was Rusty. Rusty was a beautiful, long-haired, reddish colored Spaniel that lived six doors down from us. I would often go to his yard to give him a scratch, or he would walk to my house for a visit. I would let him into our veranda or yard and make believe he was my very own. If I had to leave for school, I would lock the veranda door or latch the gate so he couldn't escape. I hoped he would be there when I got home, but he never was. Mom always let him go.

Rusty had the run of the neighborhood and would bound up to see me whenever I sat on the front steps of my house. He dropped by one Saturday morning looking like he needed help. I don't know where he had been, but he was covered in big round burdock burrs from head to toe. His beautiful, red, silky fur, wrapped around each spiky burr and he was a mess! I tried pulling the burrs out, but they wouldn't budge. The only way to get rid of those burrs was to cut them out. I went into the house, grabbed the sharp scissors from moms' sewing basket, and got to work. Rusty sat still as I cut every spikey burr out of his silky red coat. When I finished, there was a pile of red fur almost as big as Rusty himself at my feet.

You *Can't* Climb A Tree In A Dress

It was two days later when my mom approached with an angry look on her face. With an edge to her voice she asked, "Did you cut that red dog's hair? The lady down the street came to our door asking if the little girl that lives here had scalped her dog!" I told mom about Rusty being covered from head to toe in burrs, and about how I was only trying to help. Mom put her face close to mine, making me a little afraid, and in a no-nonsense sort of voice, shrieked, "Do not use scissors on any dog on our street ever again! Or any dog from anywhere!" My dog grooming days were over.

A few weeks later I was again sitting on the front porch stairs, waiting for the kids in the neighborhood to wake up. I was eager to call on one of my friends, but wasn't allowed to bother anyone so early in the morning. It delighted me when I saw my good friend Rusty bounce up the sidewalk. He was wagging his tail so fast, his whole body wiggled. His fur had grown in some, and he looked better. Thinking he might be hungry, I got up to get him a treat from the kitchen. Rusty must have really wanted to see inside, because the moment I opened the door he sped past me into the house. Mom had made it very clear that dogs were not allowed into our home. I knew she would be angry about Rusty being inside, so I ran to catch him before he wrecked anything; especially her rugs. Mom had just purchased a beautiful and costly white wool area rug for our hallway, and the living room and dining room rugs were a light cream color. Mom loved those rugs.

Rusty dashed over the new white hallway rug and into the living room and dining room. Before I could grab him, he did another quick lap, racing through the house, bumping into chairs and tables. Mom heard the racket and rushed down the stairs quicker than I had ever seen her move. "My rugs, my rugs, look at my rugs!" I had been too busy trying to grab Rusty to notice the bright red paw prints on every one of mom's precious carpets. Rusty was gushing blood from one of his paws. Looking at the amount of blood on the rugs, it seemed he might need a blood transfusion! How could one paw bleed that much? Mom shooed him right out the door. She was not the least bit concerned about Rusty and his injured foot. I wanted to follow him and help, but the look on mom's face stopped me dead in my tracks. That was not her happy face.

I loved every dog in the world except one. Pokey lived in the house across the street with the Lee family. He was a tubby black dog that waddled when he walked on his short little legs. I tried to pat him once, but he snapped, snarled, and showed me his big yellow teeth. Pokey was a grouch, which is why I never invited him into our veranda or yard like the other dogs on the street. He must have felt left out, because he invited himself over one day. It was Christmas and mom had cooked a delicious turkey dinner. We had barely made a dent in the huge bird, so mom set the hot turkey in the veranda to keep cool until she could get around to it later that evening. We loved mom's leftover meals and looked forward to turkey sandwiches with pickles, hot turkey sandwiches with gravy, turkey soup, turkey salad, turkey with noodles, and turkey potpie.

When mom went out to the veranda to get the turkey later that evening, she couldn't find it. Because the veranda door was slightly ajar, she looked outside. There on the sidewalk, munching on our Christmas turkey, lay that fat dog Pokey. That rotten little dog had pushed his way in and grabbed the leftover turkey, making off with two weeks' worth of meals. Mom was furious! That traitor Pokey had ruined my chances of ever getting a dog...

It Was an Experiment

I related better to dogs than cats. It's not that I didn't like cats, I simply liked dogs better. Kenny told me that cats and dogs were natural enemies and did not get along. This was news to me and made me curious. I wondered what would happen if you put a dog and a cat together. Kenny came up with the bright idea of trying it out. He would hold a dog and I would hold a cat. We would bring the two of them together and watch what happens. It would be an experiment, he said.

It did not take long to round up a stray cat on the street. I picked up the squirming grey cat and gripped it tight. Kenny picked up his new dog Rufus and cradled him in his arms. We were ready to begin.

It was a short experiment, because as soon as I had the cat in my arms and close to the dog's face, it went berserk! The cat spat and growled, thrust out his nails, and clawed his way up and over my face, before leaping to the ground and scurrying away. That out of control, crazy cat, scratched and tore up my face from my forehead down to my chin. He had clawed up inside my nose and blood was gushing out! I headed home for help. Mom took one look at me and almost fainted. She demanded to know what had happened, so I explained it like this, "I was holding a cat, and Kenny was holding a dog. The cat turned into a wildcat and attacked me!" I thought it best to leave out the part about it being an experiment.

Mom lifted me up on the kitchen counter and cleaned my wounds with peroxide and iodine. She pinched my nose to stem the bleeding and declared, "That cat could have scratched your eyes out!" She might have been right. Those long razor-sharp claws had come awful close to my eyes. That was such a bad idea Kenny had...

Can You Fix Our Bird?

Valerie and I were playing in the front street when we saw a beautiful Robin Red Breast fluttering in distress. He was struggling to fly but one wing didn't seem to work. All he could do was turn in a little circle on the grass. We didn't know what to do, so picked him up and brought him in to Valerie's mom. After a quick examination she established the robin had a broken wing. When we asked if she could fix it she hesitated, glancing first at the bird, and then at our concerned faces. Promising to try her best, she gathered up a few supplies and arranged them on the kitchen table. Using tape and small wooden pieces, she gently splinted his injured wing. Valarie's mom filled a shoebox with soft padding and placed our robin inside to rest and heal.

I went often to Valerie's house to check on our little friends' progress. He did not look overjoyed, but he was still alive. I was positive he would be okay. It was many days before Valerie's mom decided it was time to set him free. Valerie ran to my door to tell me that, today was the day. I would not have missed it for the world!

We gathered in the backyard and Valerie's mom tipped the shoebox, slipping our little bird onto the grass. We stayed far back so as not to frighten him. He flapped his injured wing, testing it out. I held my breath as he flapped both wings and inched forward. With a pounding heart I willed him onward, hoping against hope for him to spread those beautiful wings and soar up to the sky.

It might have been a storybook ending if not for that horrible grey cat that had clawed my face in the "dog meets cat experiment" a few weeks earlier. Perched on the corner of Valerie's backyard fence, sat that grey cat. Much to our horror, and before we could do anything to stop it, that mangy cat pounced at lightning speed from the fence to the ground. Our poor little robin did not stand a chance. None of us were quick enough to save him.

I left Valerie's yard without saying goodbye. I knew I would never forget what had happened to that defenceless little bird. This was not the ending I had hoped for and I was heartbroken. I felt horrible and cried for a long time.

I did not like that cat...

Mom Was Not a Big Fan of Cats

Mom was not partial to cats. I don't know what her exact reasons were, but she freaked out whenever she saw one. It was during a family road trip to British Columbia that I got to witness the actual extent of that fear.

We were travelling along the highway when the van in front of us flipped over onto its side and skidded down the middle of the road. Dad slammed on the brakes, stopping within inches of the overturned vehicle. He jumped out to see if anyone in the van was hurt. From our open window we could hear the lone male driver of the van telling dad he had fallen asleep at the wheel. The man was in a state of shock after his abrupt wake-up call, but unharmed and able to wriggle out through the side window. Several cars and trucks stopped to assist, creating a huge traffic jam on the highway. A burly man from one of the big trucks suggested they attach a chain to the van and pull it upright.

Suddenly, the gentleman from the van shouted, "My cat!" He had forgotten that his cat was in the overturned vehicle. My sister Rose and I had a great view from the backseat of our car and watched as the man retrieved an extremely agitated Siamese cat from the overturned van. Clutching the squirming cat in his arms, and struggling to control it, he made his way over to our car. Because mom's window was wide open, he plopped the cat right onto her lap. Mom let out a blood-curdling scream, grabbed the cat and flung it out the window! That guy's beloved cat went sailing through the air! The horrified man could not believe what our mom had just done. To tell you the truth, Rose and I could not believe it either. Our sweet mother, the one who made it her life's mission to upset no one, the one who was always so gracious and kind to strangers, the one who was always willing to help anyone and everyone, had sent this man's precious cat flying. It was a sight to behold, and hilarious when viewed from our vantage point in the backseat. Rose and I looked at each other and burst out laughing.

The cat scurried away, and the man appeared horrified. Our shaken mother apologized profusely to the gentleman, explaining her tremendous fear of cats. She assured him that her daughters in the backseat would gladly help him round up his cat and hold on to it while he tended to his vehicle. He seemed very hesitant, but agreed…

Free Fish

Kenny and I were at the new pet store in Polo Park Shopping Centre the day it opened. As a gift for visiting the store, they were giving a free goldfish to each customer. We approached the counter and were each handed a tiny goldfish in a small plastic bag of water. We stashed those in our jacket pockets and got in line for two more. This was so easy, we thought we would try for as many as they cared to give us. It was harder to hide four bags of fish, so I kept watch over them outside the store while Kenny stood in line again. He returned with our fifth little fish. No one much cared that the same kids were continuing to come back again and again, so we kept doing it until we had a grand total of fourteen tiny bags of goldfish. We could not believe our good fortune.

We struggled home with all those little bags, making many stops along the way. By the time we arrived at my house, Kenny confessed it wasn't likely his mom would let him keep his share of the fish. I jumped at his offer to take them all.

Kenny helped me carry the fourteen bags into my house where we spread them out onto the hallway floor. Overjoyed, I called out, "Mom, come and see what I have!"

Mom saw the fourteen fish in the bags but said nothing. Her awe and delight at my good fortune, seemed to have rendered her speechless. She eventually asked, "What is all this?"

I could barely contain my excitement as I explained, "The pet store gave Kenny and me fourteen fish for free, and Kenny doesn't want his." Mom did not seem to grasp what I was telling her so I added, "They're ours!" That cleared things up but did not make her happy.

"Where on earth are we going to put all these goldfish? What were you thinking? Were you even thinking at all?" Mom was not as thrilled with these fish as I was.

Dad heard the commotion and came to see what was going on. Dad was the most patient and understanding man in the world and always had a great attitude about things. Solving problems was something he was good at. He went to the basement and came back with the big five-gallon mason urn mom made her mustard pickles in. After filling it with water, he dropped our fourteen new friends into their temporary home. A short time later dad built a small cement fishpond in the backyard, and the fish loved it!

The fish had grown at least three times their size by the end of the summer. With winter coming on the pond would freeze solid, so it was back to the mustard pickle vat.

All fourteen survived the winter and returned to the freedom of the backyard fishpond the following summer…

Little Myrtle

I continued to pester my mother daily for the dog I desperately wanted, but she would not give in. Dad asked if I would like to have a small turtle as a pet instead. I wasn't sure how he made the leap from dog to turtle, but it sounded like it might be fun. I did not know of any other kids having their own turtle, and I loved the idea of having something unique.

Dad drove me to the pet store and let me choose the turtle I liked best. I was not sure what a good turtle even looked like, so I just pointed at one and hoped for the best. The pet store guy picked up my turtle and put her in a small white box with tiny holes. He tucked in the top flaps of the box and set it in my hands. We bought turtle food in an orange tin, a small glass bowl, and colored gravel. All the way home I held the box up to my eye, peering at my new friend through the tiny air holes. I asked dad to help me choose a good turtle name, and he suggested Myrtle. Myrtle the turtle... I loved it!

Myrtle was the size of a silver dollar. I always thought turtles dawdled, but Myrtle could motor impressively fast on those short little legs and proved to be quite entertaining. She would run from one hand to the other, over and over. It was fun having a turtle, and I took good care of her. I cleaned her bowl and fed her every day from the orange tin. I loved that little green turtle with the pretty painted bottom shell.

Disaster struck one warm spring day. I was home from school for lunch. After eating a quick bowl of soup, I carried Myrtle out to the backyard to play in the little cement fishpond. She swam for a bit and then climbed up onto the bricks along the sides of the pond. Mom called from the house to say it was time for me to get back to school. Myrtle seemed content sunning herself on the brick, and I hated to spoil her fun. I wasn't sure about leaving her, but school would be over in a few short hours and I would be back no time. I shouted goodbye to Myrtle and dashed off to school.

Once school let out, I ran as fast as I could to get home. Mighty Mouse started at 4:00, and I didn't want to miss one minute of my favorite television show. I raced through the backyard gate and stopped at the pond to grab Myrtle. The brick she had been on earlier was empty. I searched the pond, the grass, the garden and every other nook and cranny in the yard. Myrtle had disappeared.

I ran into the house to ask if mom had seen Myrtle anywhere. "Well, she must be in her bowl" she replied. I told her I had left Myrtle outside while I was at school and she was not in the yard any longer. To mom's credit she did not say a word about my poor judgement. Realizing how upset I was, she kept those thoughts to herself. Mom joined me in the backyard and helped search. We searched under every leaf, through every blade of grass, behind the green rowboat propped up against the garage and under the back porch, but Myrtle was nowhere to be found. When dad got home from work, he too did a thorough search.

It broke dad's heart to tell me Myrtle was gone for good. Dad was always able to come up with explanations that made you feel better about bad things though. He sat me down and told me he had a good idea about what had happened. Dad believed that Myrtle, with those speedy little legs of hers, must have slipped between the slats in our fence, zoomed down the back lane to the schoolyard, cut across the playground, and scurried across the two lanes of traffic on Wolseley Avenue. After safely crossing the road, she would have strolled through the yard of one of the big houses that backed onto the river, scrambled down the steep riverbank, and slipped into the Assiniboine river. Dad was positive Myrtle had made many new friends and was surely having the time of her life.

I missed Myrtle, and felt sad about her leaving, but I didn't cry. I liked the story dad told and believed it was true. Dad always knew things other people didn't. I loved my dad for that...

"Harry, She Doesn't Want that Turtle!"

It was probably because dad felt bad about Myrtle running away from home that he surprised me one day. He had been away on a fishing trip and arrived home with a cardboard box. I rushed over, eager to see what was inside. Dad drew up the flaps of the cardboard box to reveal a huge turtle. This turtle was the size of a dinner plate. Its long claws scraped against the cardboard and two beady little black eyes sized me up. This turtle was creepy and nothing like my little, silver dollar sized Myrtle. Mom was not the slightest bit impressed and shouted, "Harry, she does not want that turtle, get it out of the house!" Mom was right, I did not want that turtle. I also didn't want my dad to think I didn't appreciate his gift, which is why I heard myself say, "Mom, I love the turtle and want to keep him." What a big fat whopper that was.

It rained the following day, and dad suggested I take my new turtle out to the front lawn so he could enjoy the rain and have a run. I preferred he remained in his box forever with the lid on tight. Not wanting to disappoint my dad, I picked up the box and headed for the front door. That monster turtle made scary scratching noises on the cardboard, and I was scared he would burst through the box. I did not feel good about this and wished I had told dad the truth. I dumped the box on the lawn, lifted the lid, and tipped the turtle out. He seemed angry, so I jumped out of his way. He was moving quickly and making a beeline straight for the road. I did not want him to get hit by a car, but was scared to touch him with my hands, so I nudged him with my foot. Every time I inched him forward, he would move his powerful legs and run back the other way. He was very stubborn, and we were not making much progress. After much prodding and pushing, I finally got him back onto the grass and into the box. Sealing the lid tight, I carried him back to the veranda. I did not like this turtle and didn't know what to do about it.

I'm not sure if my dad had been watching me from the window, or if he just knew, but the next day the box was empty and the turtle was gone. When I asked dad where the turtle disappeared to, all he said was… the river. I asked no more questions, and dad gave no more explanation. I'm glad my dad knew me well enough to know the truth about my pretending to love that turtle.

I worried about little Myrtle though, and hoped she would be safe sharing the river with that big, beady-eyed freak, with the long creepy claws…

Oscar the First

Mom and I hopped on the Portage Avenue street car headed for Downtown. We were off to Eaton's Department Store. It was always fun going to Eaton's because it was enormous and seemed like an adventure. After browsing for a while, we finished up in my favorite part of the store, the pet department. A cage loaded with friendly little hamsters was the first thing I saw. I stuck my hand into the enclosure to pat them. One grouchy hamster must have been having a bad day, because he bit my finger, making it bleed. The others appeared harmless enough, so I asked mom if I could have one. My pitch went something like this, "May I have a hamster? May I please have a hamster? May I please, please, please, have a hamster?" This never worked when petitioning for a dog, so I wasn't expecting her to answer yes. To my surprise, she responded yes, I could come back with my dad on the weekend and choose one. I couldn't believe my ears!

After telling dad the great news, he went to work building a small cage for our new friend. He made it out of wood and lined it with aluminum. It had a wire mesh front and a tiny door that locked when it shut. Dad created a small running wheel for exercise and placed cedar chips on the floor. It was ready to go. The only thing missing was the hamster.

When the weekend arrived, we hopped in the car and drove to Eaton's. Once inside the store we headed straight for the elevator. The elevator was right beside the giant, bronze Timothy Eaton statue, which I loved. Dad pushed the elevator button, and we hopped in. The uniformed operator wore white gloves. He asked what floor we wanted and pushed the big lever forward to make the elevator climb. When the door opened on the sixth floor, we walked straight to the pet area. The hamster display case was right where I remembered. Dad had a quick peek at all the hamsters and told me to pick whichever one I wanted. There were a lot of hamsters scurrying around the display case and it was tough to choose. I was having a hard time deciding, so asked my dad for his help. Dad pointed to a hamster and said, "If I was choosing, I would pick him. He looks like a good one". The hamster my dad pointed at was brown, with two little black eyes, a little pink nose, soft fuzzy fur, and a friendly little face. He looked the same as all the other hamsters. I don't know why dad chose him, but if he liked him, that was good enough for me. Dad always noticed things other people didn't, and I trusted him. That is how Oscar the first, came to live with our family. We had no idea how much trouble that one little rodent would cause.

Dad was good at making things, so shoddy workmanship was not the reason the wheel squeaked when Oscar ran on it. (which he did, all night, every night). Apparently, hamsters are nocturnal and come to life when the rest of the house is trying to sleep. Dad tried oiling the wheel the first night and greasing it the next. No amount of adjusting, greasing, or oiling helped, and the annoying squeak continued. Also, the latch on the cage door may have been faulty as I woke up one morning to an open door and an empty cage. Dad had left for work, so my sisters, mom and I hunted. Mom had an intense fear of mice. This hamster was no different from a mouse as far as it concerned her. As long as Oscar was locked securely in his cage, my mom could tolerate having him in the house, but when she heard he was loose, she freaked out! Nobody would leave the house until we found him. We went through all the obvious hiding places, but Oscar had vanished.

When dad got home from work, he joined the search. Dad predicted Oscar was curled up in a dark corner, sleeping the day away. He supposed Oscar would wake up hungry, return to his cage looking for food and remain there.

Oscar returned to his cage to eat and drink each night, but he did not stick around. After having his fill, he would return to roaming the house at will. Mom refused to relax until we found Oscar and locked him up. Several days and nights went by before we located my wayward hamster. We found him curled up and sound asleep in my sister's boot. Mom could sleep once again. This was the first of many times Oscar escaped. I was actually a little impressed with his Houdini like skills.

There came a time when Oscar's quest for freedom got him into serious trouble. We were leaving for the lake. The car was packed and ready to go so I hurried to grab Oscar. My heart sank when I saw the empty cage. My family was eager to be off to the lake, but joined me in the hunt. We combed the whole house from top to bottom, but could not find Oscar anywhere. Dad decided we had no choice but to leave without him. We placed food and water on the kitchen floor and left Oscar to fend for himself. I left with a heavy heart and hoped Oscar would be okay while I was gone.

Oscar never made it back to his cage. Dad found Oscar in the basement. He must have slipped through the basement stairs onto the hard, concrete floor. He was alive, but could not move his back legs. Dad knew how much I loved Oscar and tried to postpone the inevitable by constructing a little wagon which attached to his back end. It worked, but Oscar seemed in a great deal of pain. Dad decided the wagon wasn't the kindest solution, so put Oscar out of his misery. When dad broke the news, I was broken-hearted and cried for a long time. Mom tried to console me, suggesting I could have another hamster. My sincere, but rather dramatic response was, "I don't want another hamster, I only want Oscar!" My poor parents did not know what to do about that.

Time has a way of healing all wounds and I agreed to look for another hamster. I was certain I could not find another hamster half as perfect as my much-loved Oscar, but I was mistaken about that. Oscar was the first of seven hamsters I would own as a kid, and I named every one of them Oscar. The Oscars, one through seven, all lived remarkable lives, and I loved them all. Each one was unique, and each had their own peculiar tale to tell, about living with a little girl making do with a hamster, when what she really wanted was a dog…

Best Day Ever

After years of begging mom for a dog, I wore her down. It was during a weak moment, and I took advantage of the situation. Something must have been going on that day because she seemed preoccupied and upset. She did not seem herself, and I am sure the last thing she wanted to hear was my whining about a dog. I saw this as a golden opportunity and started with the familiar refrain of, "May I have a dog? Please may I have a dog? Why can't I have a dog?" She snapped and shouted, "Oh go get a dog, I don't care!" I could not believe my ears. It was like Christmas, birthday, and the last day of school all rolled into one. Because of this sudden outburst, and what seemed like confirmation, I ran to the backyard and called to dad, "Mom says we can have a dog!" Dad replied, "Well let's go find one." I don't recall him going into the house to check with my mom to make sure I hadn't heard wrong. The way I remember it, we hopped in the car and off we went to the dog pound in search of a dog. Dad wanted a dog almost as much as I did, so I assume they had discussed the matter earlier, which may have accounted for mom's irritation.

We were on our way to get a dog and I could hardly contain myself. I had visions of countless strays lined up in rows of cages, wagging their tails, imploring me to take them home. That was far from what happened though. There were only a handful of dogs at the dog pound and they were not the least bit friendly. Most of them acted as if they wanted to eat me! It was a huge disappointment, but we still had the humane society to visit. I hopped back in the car hoping to have better luck there.

A cheerful man greeted us at the door of the humane society, and led us to the back room where the dog runs were. There were close to ten dogs of varying sizes, breeds, and colors to choose from. I studied each dog as I made my way down the row. The last cage held an unusual looking black dog. The man said many people had met this little dog, but no one wanted to take her. He kept her longer than was normal because he had grown fond of her. She was not what you would call beautiful. She was an odd mix of several breeds, with short little legs, a long body, wiry coat, drooping ears, and extra-long whiskers. She was a rather strange looking little thing. I got down on my knees and waited for her to come. She approached and looked me in the eyes. I did not say a word, I just observed. I was not sure what I was even searching for, but I was certain I would know it when I saw it... and I did. This unusual little dog, had the kindest, friendliest brown eyes I had ever seen. They were gentle, intelligent, loyal eyes, eyes that melted your heart. Dad must have noticed those eyes also, or perhaps something in my eyes, because he concluded she was the one. This delighted the man that had shown her to us. He said she would have to be spayed, so it would be a few days before we could take her home. There are no words to describe how excited I felt. I did not know how it would be possible to wait three days to have her at home with us. Dad paid the man for the operation, plus a small purchase fee, and it was official, she was mine. We named her Whiskers, which suit her perfectly.

The wait was agonizing. I put food and water bowls on the kitchen floor and mom contributed an old comforter that would serve as a comfy little dog bed. Several cans of dog food sat waiting on the shelf. All that was missing was my dog.

Dad must have taken time from work to pick Whiskers up from the Animal Hospital because she was waiting in our kitchen when I arrived home from school. I entered through the back door and heard excited barking. There in my very own kitchen, was that little black dog I had fallen in love with two days earlier. Her shaved tummy exposed a long row of black stitches from the surgery, but I felt she was the most perfect dog I had ever seen. She came over, tail wagging, delighted to see me. I had my very own dog, and she was ten thousand times better than any canary, goldfish, turtle, or hamster.

Whiskers was eager to please and learned new tricks easily. She came running when called, or at the sound of the dog whistle. We trained her to roll over, play dead, shake a paw, stay, retrieve a ball, sneeze on command, and say her prayers. I would lay her favorite treat on her nose and she would remain glued in place until commanded to release it. She would toss the treat high into the air and catch it in her mouth every time. When it was wet outside, she would come in the back door and wait on the mat until we showed up with a cloth to dry her feet. She would lift one foot at a time until we cleaned each paw. My Aunt Rosa, who knew how much I loved dogs, knit a beautiful, bright red, dog sweater for her. It arrived in the mail all the way from Arizona, and was addressed to, "Miss Whiskers Brooks". That red sweater kept Whiskers toasty warm on the many cold wintery Winnipeg walks we enjoyed together.

Whiskers seemed to appreciate the fact we had rescued her. I always felt she was trying her absolute hardest to please us. She may not have won any beauty pageants, but she was a perfect little dog. My whole family fell in love with her. I always suspected Whiskers was trying, just a little harder, to win my mother's approval. Mom, who never cared for dogs and did not want one in our home, found it impossible to resist Whiskers' gentle, loving charm. She grew to love and adore that puppy as much as the rest of us. Whiskers was an easy dog to have around and mom seemed to welcome the company when she was home alone all day. It was touching to see the bond between the two of them develop. Whiskers wasn't only my dog, she was everyone's dog–a much-loved member of our entire family...

The Lady in a Wheelchair and a Moving Truck

Five doors down from our home, and right beside the house with the stuffed moose head on the veranda, lived an old woman in a wheelchair. Her name was Susie. Kenny and I would visit with her when she was sitting in her veranda. She was a nice lady, but her conversations were a little boring, and she smelled funny, so we never stuck around long.

One afternoon we spotted a moving truck outside of Susie's home. A gentleman was hauling furniture out of Susie's house and placing it into a truck. It looked as if Susie was moving, so we ran to check it out. The truck was like nothing we had ever seen. It looked like the type of covered wagon you would see in a Western movie, with its rounded metal spines and white canvass. Kenny and I hopped on and off the truck, checking out every piece of furniture placed inside. When we stood on the tables and chairs, we could reach the curved metal spine. We were having a great time using it as a monkey bar. It was while we were swinging from the metal bar that the truck started up and drove away. Turning a corner was exciting because we would sway wildly from one side and then to the other. The faster the truck moved, the more fun it was. This was better than any playground equipment we had ever been on. We were having so much fun, it didn't occur to us to get off the truck before we travelled too far from home.

It was a while before we parted the canvas and peeked out the rear of the truck. It shocked us to discover we were downtown, outside Eaton's Department Store, and a long way from home. We needed to get off, but how do you jump from a moving truck onto the busiest street in Winnipeg? As were pondering our options, the truck came to a sudden stop. We took advantage of this, hopping out the back and racing across the road. Car horns blasted as we wove our way between the traffic over to the sidewalk. We were a long way from Newman Street and it was close to dinnertime. Kenny and I started running.

I made it home but had missed dinner, and mom was not happy. Our family always ate dinner together and my vacant chair had not gone unnoticed. Mom reprimanded me for being late, but did not inquire as to my whereabouts. I breathed a sigh of relief. It was one thing to avoid mentioning what I had been up to, and quite another to have to explain…

"And He Shall Give His Angels Charge Over You"

On the corner of Portage Avenue and Erin Street was a giant billboard, advertising McGavins bread. There was an open loaf of bread on one end of the billboard, and a giant toaster on the opposite end. Several long arms protruding over the top of the billboard spun around like a gigantic windmill. On the end of each of these windmill arms was a giant piece of bread. When the arms turned it appeared as if the bread pieces were leaving the open bag and popping into the toaster. This billboard was a huge attraction to us kids. We loved watching the bread go around, moving from bag to toaster.

It was during one of these visits that Kenny found a way of getting inside the billboard where all the machinery, gears and moving parts were, and I followed. Inside we watched the giant wheel with the huge sprockets turn around and around, making the long arms with the big pieces of bread on the ends pass by. It was fascinating, and I could not resist the urge to grab on to one of those arms. I took hold of the next piece of bread and rode it slowly upward. I was practically to the top before a trace of common sense kicked in... albeit a little late. The arm with the bread attached was lifting me up and into the toaster. I could continue all the way around and pop into the toaster, or let go and drop the considerable distance to the ground. Neither option seemed good, but letting go seemed the best...so I did.

I plunged straight down and hit the packed clay with a thud, barely missing the whirling gears and machinery. My body hurt all over and it was painful to breathe. The abrupt stop on the hard ground had knocked the wind out of me, and I was dazed. Kenny crouched down beside me and didn't say a word. It was a long time before I felt able to sit up. My whole body hurt and I wasn't feeling good.

On the slow walk home we chatted about all the cool stuff we had discovered inside the bread sign. We talked about my ride on the gigantic piece of bread, and wondered what would have happened if I had popped into the toaster. We were certain it would not have ended well. I'm so glad I let go when I did...

Must Have Been an Old Wire

The May long weekend was coming up and dad was taking my sister Rose and me fishing. We were taking the boat and the tent, and all the camping gear. I could hardly wait. I felt it might be a good idea to get some fishing practice in before the trip, so I hunted through the basement for my fishing rod. It took a while, but I found my rod with the red reel, along with the plastic tackle box my Uncle Stanley and Aunt Grace had given me for Christmas a few years back.

I was home from school on lunch break and only had a few minutes before I had to get back for the afternoon. I rushed out to the street with my fishing rod and tied a heavy black rubber weight to the end of the line. Ready to start, I flung my arm back and let it fly! It was a good cast. For my second cast, I brought my arm back even further. I released the button on the reel at just the right moment, freeing the line and sending the weight soaring. It was a fabulous cast! The heavy rubber weight soared through the air... and wrapped around the power line on the other side of the street. I gave a gentle tug, but it would not budge. I pulled harder, but it still wouldn't come loose. I yanked on the line with all my might, creating a loud explosion! Sparks flew everywhere, as the live, crackling wire, floated to the middle of the road.

Miss Purdy, a crabby old lady that did not like kids at the best of times, was ambling past just at that moment. She shook her cane at me and shouted some terrible things. Mrs. McDonald, the nice lady across the street from my house, heard the commotion and rushed out to see what was going on. Other neighbors soon joined her, wondering why their power had gone off.

A car coming down the street was nearing the live wire so Mrs. McDonald ran out to stop it. Another neighbor flagged down a truck coming from the other direction. Mom appeared right at that moment. She looked at the broken wire attached to my fishing line, and then at me. She put two and two together and looked as if she wanted to die.

It was time for me to get back to school, so I quickly explained the situation. I told mom it was a freak accident and that I would never purposely pull a live wire down. I then skedaddled out of there. I felt bad leaving mom all alone to handle the crisis. She hated being the center of attention and did not do well with trouble of any kind.

When I got home from school, mom told me that our neighbor, Mrs. Hall, was very upset with me. Mrs. Hall's daughter Mattie was getting married on the weekend and her wedding cake had been baking in the oven when the power went off. It was a fruitcake, and she had marinated the fruit for days. I had ruined her wedding cake. Mom made me to go to Mrs. Hall's house and tell her how very sorry I was about pulling down the power line.

I honestly was genuinely sorry. I didn't mean to pull down the wire, and I sure didn't want to wreck Mattie's wedding cake. I walked over to Mrs. Hall's house and told her how bad I felt, and how sorry I was. She was nice about it and did not seem to hate me. I came back home and told mom that Mrs. Hall had forgiven me. Mrs. Hall was such a nice lady.

It was two days after and I could not find my fishing rod anywhere. I asked mom if she knew where it was. The last place I recalled seeing it was on the street, tangled around that wire. Mom's face, and the look in her eyes, let me know that it might have been a bit soon for me to be asking about that fishing rod. Being the clever little kid I was, I did not ask a second time...

A Tree a Rope and a River

The Assiniboine River was close to where I lived and we often went to Omen's Creek to ride our bikes and to watch the river. There was a giant tree on the riverbank and one of its branches reached far out over the river. Someone had attached a long rope from the branch so you could hold on and swing out over the fast-moving water. We were all taking turns, and having a wonderful time, when I heard a voice in the distance yelling, "Maureen, you will drown in the river if you fall off!" I looked across the creek and up to the top of the hill to see who was hollering at me. I spotted Mrs. McCord, one of our neighbors from Newman Street. I was having way too much fun to stop what I was doing. I knew that Mrs. McCord worried needlessly, so I waved and shouted, "Hello Mrs. McCord, it's okay, I can swim!" Assuming I had convinced her she no longer needed to worry about me, I went back to what I was doing and carried on with the fun.

Mrs. McCord however, was not the least bit convinced. She marched directly back to Newman Street and straight to my mother, telling her what I was up to, and what I had said. My poor mother dreaded neighbors coming to our door with news of my shenanigans.

When I got home, mom demanded to know what on earth I was doing swinging on a rope over the river! I explained that it was not dangerous, and that I was in fact a great swimmer. Mom closed her eyes and took a slow deep breath, the way she often did when dealing with me. She shook her head from side to side, and used her scary voice to say, "Stay away from the river! Do not swing from ropes! Listen, when spoken to by a neighbor!" and "If you know what's good for you, you will do as you are told!"...

Police Trouble

I had several aunts which I loved and enjoyed. Two of those aunts were especially entertaining, and it was extra fun when they visited. Auntie Grace was from Vancouver, and Auntie Rosa lived in Arizona. They were dad's sisters, and they often stayed with us for a good part of the summer. Dad was the second youngest of five siblings. Family members often pointed out my resemblance to Auntie Rosa. They told many great stories about Auntie Rosa and her childhood, and I loved them all. I especially loved the story they told about her as a little girl, climbing to the top of a telephone pole in her brand-new dress. Her dress got caught on a nail on the way down and ripped. Knowing she would be in serious trouble, she removed the dress and hid the evidence. She did this by stuffing it down the family outhouse. Granny discovered the dress down the hole, and Auntie Rosa was in big trouble. This was one of many stories they told about her. I loved all the tales, and I enjoyed it when dads' family visited. All of them were witty, entertaining, and a joy to be around. Dad was just like them. When they were together, our home was filled with laughter, fun, and kind-hearted teasing. The Brooks family loved one another's company.

It was during one of those visits that mom and my two aunts decided to walk to the cemetery to say hello to my granny and grandpa. I did not like cemeteries, but I enjoyed being with my aunts, so I tagged along. Because they were walking too slowly for my liking, I ran on ahead. I noticed a branch from a big tree was overhanging the sidewalk and I thought it might be fun to climb the tree and drop things on them when they passed under. I hurried up the tree and shimmied out on the branch. It was a while before they appeared, so I had time to collect a large arsenal of leaves. When they walked under me, I dumped everything I had! It surprised them, but they chuckled when they realized the source of this unexpected shower of leaves.

My aunts and mom were not the only ones surprised by my little caper. A policeman was talking on the phone at the police call box, which was just beside us. The police had special phone boxes scattered around the city which only they could operate. Upon seeing this attack on three older women by a kid up a tree, he hurried over and asked my mom and aunts if they were okay. Before mom could get a word out of her mouth, my aunts spoke up saying they were not okay. They said they were upset and felt the young girl up the tree should be arrested and sent straight to jail. The policeman seemed to be a no-nonsense sort of guy and I was becoming a bit worried. Mom kept trying to intervene, but my aunts would not stop talking. The story kept getting worse. The policeman seemed angry and ordered me to come down out of the tree. At this point mom found her voice and intervened. She told the officer I was in fact her daughter, and these were my aunts. My aunts laughed and told him they were just trying to scare me. The policeman, not seeming to appreciate the humor, returned to the police call box. My aunts loved that my little prank backfired on me and thought it was hilarious. Mom however, was nervous about the policeman, and did not think it was at all funny. That policeman scared me a little too...

A Movie Theater and Some Cool Drums

There was a movie theater on Portage Avenue, just four blocks from our home. On Saturdays, my sisters and I would go there to watch the movies. It cost twenty-five cents to get in and for five cents you could buy popcorn with a little prize in the box. Often the prize was a black cardboard moustache you could clip onto your nostrils. The fun didn't last long because the moustache pinched, hurting your nose and making your eyes water. Sometimes the prize was a set of big red wax lips. They were minty flavored and you could chew those after you finished playing with them. We always kept our ticket stub because there was a draw which took place before the movie began. I once won a Black Beauty puzzle. It was the first thing I had ever won and I loved Black Beauty. Sometimes they would show cartoons the entire afternoon, and other times it would be a movie such as, Lassie, Rin Tin Tin, Zorro, Tarzan, Roy Rogers, or the Lone Ranger. I loved Saturdays because of those films. We were not happy when the movie theater closed and was bought by a music store.

As much as I didn't love the music store, there was one thing about it that caught my eye. On display in the huge picture window was a sparkly red drum set. Every time I went past I would pause and gaze at those drums. I was positive I was born to be a drummer. When I asked my mom what she thought about us getting the drum set in the window, she burst out laughing! It did not sound like mom would be changing her mind about the drum set idea, so I discussed it with my dad when he got home from work. Dad did not find the idea amusing at all. He simply replied, "Nope, we can't buy the drum set, but I will make you a pair of drumsticks." That sounded good, and I was content with that.

I continued to stop at the music store window to gaze at the red sparkly drums. One day while peering through the window, I noticed there wasn't anybody in the store. This was an excellent opportunity to get a closeup look at the drums. I strolled into the store, climbed up into the gigantic picture window, and perched on the seat of the drum set. A parade of cars sped by on Portage Avenue, the busiest road in Winnipeg. It was like performing on a big stage. With a drumstick in each hand, I banged the drums and cymbals with great enthusiasm. It was a short-lived performance because a man emerged out of a back room and shouted at me to leave the drums alone! I hopped down and ran.

I loved that I got to try out the drum set, even for such a short time. Those drums were even better than I imagined they would be. Too bad they didn't like little kids in that store…

Jesus Loves Me this I Know

Mom was a huge advocate of church and Sunday school and insisted us girls attend every Sunday. I did not love Sunday school, but I didn't hate it. What I didn't like was the outfit my mom made me wear. She would put me in a frilly dress with a crinoline, white gloves, a ridiculous hat, white stockings, and shiny black patent leather shoes. That was after she tortured me with the curling iron, which was always too hot, creating long blonde ringlets in my hair, before topping it off with a bow. I had to walk four agonizing blocks to the church dressed in that finery. My sister Rose loved being dressed up and delighted at parading around town in her fancy attire. I would bolt out of church the second it was over and hurry home to get out of those silly clothes. Sometimes I would not even wait to get home. I would start to undress as soon as I reached the end of our street. Off would come the hat and gloves, and the zipper on my dress would be down by the time I hit our front door. I'd run up the stairs to my bedroom and toss my Sunday school clothes onto the bed.

There was a whole year I didn't have to go to Sunday school. I could not believe it when the head of the Sunday school department suggested I take a year off. Who gets booted out of Sunday school? You would think church might be a good place for someone like me. I wasn't bad; I was just bored. It was agonizing sitting still and listening to the white-haired lady drone on, in her slow as molasses voice. She was not the least bit enthusiastic about the Bible stories she was sharing, and it was hard for me to stay focused. I must have been a terrible disruption to the church faithful because they asked Mr. Currie, the head elder, to visit my mom and convince her I should not come back to Sunday school for a year. This mortified my shy, introverted mother, who dreaded anything or anyone, calling attention to our family.

Mom wanted me at church and was not about to give up. She insisted I continue to have some involvement and signed me up with the Explorers group. Explorers were a group of girls that met at the church on Tuesday evenings. When mom informed me I would attend Explorers, I was ecstatic and could not wait for Tuesday to come. A group of girls going exploring sounded like something right up my alley. I had read some Nancy Drew books and loved the intriguing mysteries and wild adventures that involved Nancy. I secretly longed to be Nancy Drew and hoped that Explorers would be something like that. Tuesday arrived, and I flew out of the house, running the whole way to the church. The group was meeting in the church basement. I found the room and my fellow Explorers and sat down to join the twelve girls sitting around in a circle. The girls were wearing matching white shirts and blue pants. Some had red, yellow, and blue stars stitched on the arm of their white shirts. I wanted one of those outfits and some of those cool stars. I could not wait to find out where we would go exploring. Our leader welcomed me to the group and began the evening with a prayer. That seemed like a good idea; exploring was probably risky. Our leader stood and said, "Tonight we will explore the Book of Matthew, I hope you all brought your Bibles." The Bible? No, I hadn't brought a Bible. You mean we weren't going outside? My mom had neglected to mention it was the Bible we would be exploring. Tuesdays would be nothing at all like I had expected…

A Train Bridge and Poor Choices

The train tracks were a big attraction for the kids in my neighborhood. We often put pennies on the tracks and waited for a train to pass and flatten them. As the last car rumbled by, we would wave at the man in the caboose and he would wave back. We would then rush to the tracks to retrieve our flattened pennies, which were warm to touch. Sometimes we would bring the same penny back another day, making it even thinner.

A train bridge crossed over the Assiniboine River at Omens Creek. We often played on that bridge. Tall cement pillars, standing high above the river, supported the railroad tracks. Most of the wooden railway ties were set an exact distance apart from each other. There were however, two wooden ties that were narrower and set a little further apart than the rest. These two ties made for a wider space above one of the cement pillars. We were small enough to fit through the space, so one by one we squeezed through, dropping onto the open platform below the train tracks.

We were enjoying the view of the river below us when we heard a rumbling sound off in the distance. This rumbling quickly turned into a deafening roar. The bridge and pillar we were standing on rattled and shook as a massive train passed over our heads. There was nothing to hold on to and we had to sit to keep from shaking off into the river below. We had a clear view of the undercarriage of the heavy train as it passed a few feet above our heads. The noise it made was tremendously loud, and we were scared stiff. We hadn't bargained on a train coming down the tracks and it seemed to take forever for the last car to pass over.

We were anxious to get out of there, but going back up proved to be a problem. Because we had dropped a fair distance down onto the cement platform, we could not reach the wooden railway ties above to pull ourselves back up. There was nothing to stand on and the wooden ties were too high to reach. We feared being stuck there forever, before Kenny came up with an idea. He got down on his hands and knees and we used his back as a step stool. After much straining and struggling, we were able to squeeze back up to the tracks. Everyone made it but Kenny. He was the last one standing on the pillar below with no one to boost him up. Margo offered to run home and return with a rope, but Kenny did not want to stay on that pillar one second longer. One boy laid on the tracks and stretched his arms down as far as they would go, while some other kids held his feet. Grabbing Kenny's outstretched hands, he tugged with all his might until Kenny made it up and out. Kenny looked like he was about to cry.

Nobody said much on the walk home. Our little stunt was foolish and dangerous and we could have been killed. That was such a dumb thing we had done...

Exodus 20:8 "Thou Shalt Not Steal"

When Polo Park Shopping Centre first opened in 1959, it was an open-air mall. Margo and I walked over one Sunday to check it out. Stores were closed on Sundays, so there were no people mulling about. In the heart of Polo Park was a huge fountain with water gushing up and out. We were enjoying watching the water shoot up when we spotted a bunch of pennies, nickels and dimes, lying just below the surface of the water. I asked Margo why anyone would leave money lying there in the open like that. She said people threw money into the water before making a wish. She claimed the money did not belong to anybody once it was thrown away. That sort of made sense, so we filled our pockets with all the pennies, nickels and dimes within our reach. With our pockets wet and sagging, we headed off to the Bowling Alley where we bought pop and candy bars.

I may have been a rather mischievous kid who occasionally exhibited bad judgement, but I was actually very honest. I was not feeling good about this sudden windfall, and I felt guilty. The pop and candy did not taste as good as I expected it would, and I knew deep down we had done something wrong.

I never forgot about taking that money from the fountain as a kid. No matter how many years passed, it always niggled at me. That is why, many years later as an adult, I made a return trip to that fountain. My three young children were with me and were shocked to see me throwing a handful of dollar coins into the water, one at a time. They did not know what had come over me. They ran over to their father to inform him, "Mom is throwing a whole bunch of loonies into the fountain!" I laughed, but did not give an explanation. That was a story for another day.

I made no wishes when I threw those coins into that fountain but I got something wonderful in return; a clear conscience…

On Your Mark, Get Set, Go!

My sisters and I shared two pair of figure skates that had been in our family for years. They were well used but looked pretty good after a coat of white polish and new white laces. Both pair of skates were large, so we had to wear several layers of socks to make them fit our feet. This wasn't a bad thing, as Winnipeg winters were cold and the rinks were all outdoors. It was often thirty or forty below zero, but the frigid weather never kept us away from the rink. We loved skating and would bundle up and skate almost every day at the outdoor rink a block from our home. If my dad was home, we would have him tie our skates because he could always get them tighter than we could. We would then walk to the rink with our skates on, or skate part of the way there on the icy back lane.

There was a little wooden shed at the rink where you could put your skates on, or warm up. A roaring fire in the wood stove kept it toasty warm. The kids called the man that kept the fire burning, Pop. He also cleared the snow off the rink. When we came inside the shed to warm up, we didn't stay longer than it took for our frozen fingers and toes to thaw. Pop did not speak a word of English and was always eating hunks of garlic sausage from the tip of a large, menacing hunting knife. He did not seem to like children and scared us a bit.

They sometimes held school gym class outdoors, and in the winter, we would skate for an hour on the rink behind the school. Because I skated almost every day, I was pretty good at it.

My gym teacher had been watching our class and called me over to ask if I was a speed skater. I was the speediest skater of all my friends, so I said yes. She informed me there was a citywide speed skating meet at the Winnipeg Arena on Friday evening, and if I wanted to compete, she would enter my name. After considering it for a moment I decided it might be fun and agreed to do it.

On Friday evening I walked the short distance to the Winnipeg Arena, carrying my skates over my shoulder. Once inside, I made my way down to ice level, and found a man with a clipboard. I told him my name, and that I was skating for Isaac Brock School. He scanned the rows of names and found mine near the bottom. He said my race was starting soon and I should hurry and get ready. I laced up my ill-fitting figure skates and hurried to the starting line.

The starter told me what lane to stand in, and we were ready to go. I did a quick glance sideways to check out my competition. The girls were all wearing actual racing clothes and black speed skates, with long blades. I was wearing a heavy winter jacket, regular pants, and figure skates. It seemed this was a real speed skating race; not a race for speedy skaters. What on earth was I doing here? Why hadn't I listened when my gym teacher was describing the race? How could I get off the ice and out of here?

But it was too late to leave, because the starter shouted, "Take your mark!" A second later the starting pistol went off with a loud bang. I had no choice but to race. Digging the pick of my skate into the ice, I took off as fast as I could. By the time we rounded the first corner I was at the front of the pack and easily keeping up with the rest of the girls. Halfway through the race I was ahead of the pack and still picking up speed. As I rounded the last corner I glanced behind to see how close the next skater was. I was ahead by at least twenty feet and glided over the finish line for an easy win.

I was happy to have won, but didn't stick around to receive my first-place medal. I was in the wrong skates and the wrong clothes, and I wanted to get out of there as quick as I could...

Hockey Night in Winnipeg

My sister Rose and I played on a girl's hockey team together. We had no hockey equipment so dad showed us how to tape magazines over our lower legs as shin pads, and he scrounged up two hockey sticks from somewhere. The coach gave us team jerseys which we pulled over our winter jackets and layers of clothing. Winnipeg winters were cold, and we played on outdoor hockey rinks, so we needed to dress warmly. Our goalie was a hefty girl who could not skate all that well. At the start of the game two girls would go on either side of her, each taking an arm, and push her across the rink. They would place her in the net where she would stand for the whole game, stopping most pucks. She was awesome! The rest of our team were great skaters and good hockey players. We competed against and beat several community teams throughout Winnipeg.

Broadway was one of the more challenging teams we played. They were a hard-hitting bunch of girls, who were more interested in knocking us down than playing the actual game. They were tough, and used language that would have made my mother declare, "They are no ladies!"

It was during a game against Broadway that an all-out brawl broke out. My sister was in the corner trying to get the puck away from one of their players. The Broadway player tripped

Rose and was kicking her while she lay sprawled on the ice. I was furious! I jumped off the bench and sped towards them. I had the Broadway player in my sites as I dropped my shoulder and slammed into her at full speed, sending her flying off of my sister. This prompted the entire Broadway team to clear the bench and pile on top of me. The whole team was punching and kicking me while Rose pounded on their backs yelling, "Leave my sister alone, leave my sister alone!" Unable to take on the whole team, I curled up into a ball, protecting my head with my arms. The weird thing was, the punches and kicks weren't hurting all that much because I had on so many layers of clothing and was quite padded. The coaches pulled everyone off and called the game.

I was disappointed we didn't get to finish the game, but I did not regret in the slightest what I had done. I would do it again if they did that to my sister. I was proud of Rose for trying to get the whole hockey team off me when they all piled on. She was tougher than I knew...

The Old, Worn Out Baseball Glove

Because I was an avid baseball player I spent hours throwing and catching balls. If I had no one to play catch with, I would throw a ball up against the garage door and catch it, over and over again. It wasn't our garage door; it was the next-door neighbor's. She had a nice cement pad and a newer door, perfect for throwing balls at. She never objected, so I did it a lot.

Wolseley School had a good baseball diamond, and we played there often. We played, work your way up baseball games for hours. Girls and boys played together, and all were welcome to join. I didn't have a baseball glove, so borrowed one from whomever was up to bat and not using theirs.

When I was asked to join the grade six girls school baseball team, I wished I owned my own glove. I was flattered they had invited me to play, because I was only in grade four, but I was nervous about asking these older girls to borrow their gloves.

A curious thing happened a few days after being invited to play on the girls grade six team. I was cutting across the empty schoolyard when I came upon a leather baseball glove sitting right in the middle of the field. It was old, soft and well used, but seemed like an okay glove. When I tried the glove on I could only insert my thumb and index finger, as the three remaining holes were jammed shut. If I kept my middle, ring, and baby finger outside of the glove, it seemed to work. I could not believe my good fortune and went home to show my mom what I had found. Mom wasn't as excited as I was. She said, "The glove is not yours, and you need to put it back where you found it." I told her that was a bad idea because someone else would come along and take it. She pondered this for a moment and agreed. Her next suggestion was, that I go to the field when all the kids were playing and ask each one if they knew whose glove it was. I agreed to this but hoped no one would claim it. At the field the next day, I asked every single kid if they knew who owned the glove. No one did, so I used it for the whole afternoon. At dinner I told mom I had asked everyone if they'd lost a glove, and no one had. She said I needed to try again the next day. The next day I asked every kid once again, but no one knew who owned the glove. I was sure I would be able to keep it, but when I told my mom that every kid at the schoolyard said they didn't lose a glove–she still wouldn't let me have it. She said I had to go back and ask again. Because I wanted to keep it, I thought it might help if I demonstrated the actual sorry condition of this baseball glove. I told her the glove was a piece of junk, and showed her the impossibility of inserting my three fingers into the squished holes. I pointed out the worn and flimsy condition of the glove, and mentioned it was lacking any padding. She looked closer and agreed that it perhaps wasn't of much value. This got me excited. I was certain she would say I could keep it. Mom however, did not agree to me keeping the glove. She said I was to continue asking if someone had lost a glove every time I went to the playground.

Mom was like that. She wanted nothing she hadn't worked for, and she would not feel right about keeping something that wasn't hers. She borrowed nothing from anyone, and hated to owe anyone anything. That old, worn out, well used baseball glove, with the squished fingers and no padding, was no different. It belonged to someone else and the right thing to do was to find the person it belonged to. I never found the owner of that old baseball glove, and I used it for many years...

The Marble Dilemma

All the kids on our street played marbles. I had a huge collection because we played for keeps, and I was a good marble player. We were very serious about our marbles and made very careful decisions about which ones we would risk losing during a game. Cat's eye marbles were abundant and not worth much. White marbles with assorted colored swirls were more valuable but still not considered rare. Crystal marbles however, were rare and treasured. Everyone knew the value of a crystal marble and rarely risked losing them in a game. Most kids had lots of the small-sized marbles, but nobody had many of the large marbles called crocks. These were precious and coveted. Some kids kept their marbles in purple cloth bags with pull strings that liquor bottles came in. My parents didn't imbibe, so I kept my marbles in one of my mom's old purses.

There was a boy on our street named Victor. I did not like him and never played with him. He was mean and a bully, and none of us kids enjoyed being around him. A group of us were playing marbles on the boulevard when Victor came up and bragged about being a great marble player. He said he could beat all of us and take all of our marbles if he wanted. Margo took exception to this and blurted, "Maureen could beat you… you should play her." I spun around and gave Margo the stink eye! Why was she getting me involved? I didn't like Victor, and I did not want to play marbles with him. But it was too late, because he accepted Margo's challenge and ran to his house to get his marbles. He was back in a flash and ready to play. The group of kids I'd been playing with circled around to watch. Victor took a crock out of his bag, which meant I had to play a crock as well. I did not like this at all. I hardly ever played my crocks because I only had a few and did not want to lose any. My least favorite crock was the cat's eye, so I played it. The game was on. To everyone's delight I won that game and Victors' crock. He insisted we keep playing so he could get his marble back. If I had lost one of my crocks, I would have stopped playing. They were too special to risk losing. I used my cat's eye crock again and won the next game as well. Victor was now down two of his crocks. We played four more games, and I won them all. I now owned six of Victor's coveted crocks. I could not believe my good fortune. What was Victor thinking? I didn't know of any other kid that would play six of their best marbles and risk losing them like that. Victor looked dejected and didn't want to play anymore. I was so excited about winning, I ran straight home to share the good news with my mom. I had the six marbles I had won in my hand and hurried to the kitchen to show her.

Mom knew nothing about marbles. To her they were all the same. She knew I had a purse full, as I often spread them out on the floor to play with and admire, but she didn't appreciate the true value of the different colors or the importance of the crocks. I was ecstatic about my winnings and wanted her to understand the magnitude of my win, so I explained the marble playing protocol to her. She listened to all I had to say and considered it for a moment before saying, "It wasn't nice of you to take all of Victor's best marbles, you need to give them back." Give them back? I didn't take them, I won them fair and square! No one gives marbles back! Mom did not understand the marble code of conduct. She could see I was upset at her suggestion and said we should wait until my father got home to see what he had to say about it.

I met my dad at the door and explained everything to him. Dad listened and came up with a solution. He said he understood that I was an excellent marble player, and that I had won the marbles fairly, but I needed to put myself in Victors' shoes. He asked how I would feel if someone had won six of my best marbles. I told him I would never have lost six crocks because I wouldn't have played them. He understood that, but wondered if by some chance I had, wouldn't I want someone to give them back? I supposed I would, but wasn't convinced. Dad thought about it for a minute and came up with a solution. He said I should ask Victor if he would like to trade me one marble of my choosing from his collection, for the six crocks. I didn't want to, but was starting to feel a tiny bit sorry for Victor.

The next day I walked down to Victor's house with the six crocks in my hand and presented my dad's idea to him. Victor seemed happy about it and agreed right away. He got his marble bag and emptied it out onto the grass so I could make my choice. Victor had a lot of cool marbles, but one stood out from all the rest. It was a crystal crock. I had seen a few before, but not many. I held out the six crocks and told Victor I would trade him all six, for the one crystal crock. He thought about it for a minute and decided it was a good trade. Victor seemed happy to get his six marbles back, and I was thrilled to be the new owner of that beautiful, sparkly, crystal crock of his. It turned out okay for both of us, and I felt good about it. That was a good idea dad had...

Sixty Seconds of Fame

One year for Christmas I received a pair of blue skis and ski poles. The Winnipeg City Dump had been shut down and made into a ski hill and park. They were having a grand opening and offering free ski lessons for kids as a way of getting people out. I didn't have ski boots to go with my skis, but dad came up with an idea. He dug out an old pair of my Granny's winter boots and tried to convince me they looked just like ski boots. The boots were short, sturdy, brown leather things that laced up. There was thick fur along the laces and around the top of the boots. They looked nothing like ski boots. They looked like a pair of your Granny's winter boots from a hundred years ago! I did not want to wear them. Dad, as always, came up with an idea. He took a sharp knife to the fur trim and got rid of it all. If you used your imagination, they did sort of look like ski boots.

With my new blue skis and Granny's old brown leather boots, my dad drove us to the opening of the brand-new ski hill. I found my ski instructor and a group of kids waiting to take instruction. After a short lesson we walked up the hill in our skis, doing the herringbone maneuver the instructor had taught us. We followed our instructor down the hill a few times doing the snow plow. He then left us to figure the rest out on our own. I went up and down the hill a thousand times that day and had the time of my life. I loved it, and planned on skiing for the rest of my life.

The launch of the new ski hill on the old City Dump was a bit of a big deal, and there were TV cameras filming it. They interviewed me on camera and filmed a short clip of me skiing down the hill. It was shown on the ten o'clock news, but I was in bed and didn't get to see it. A lot of other people had seen the news and made a point of mentioning it to my parents and me. My teacher had seen me on TV and told the class about it.

Skiing on the old City Dump had made me a star for a day. I was famous...

Ghosts, Goblins, and Mr. Blackmore

Halloween was always a lot of fun. I never put much thought into my costume and was a hobo just about every year. There were always lots of hobos, ghosts, and pirates running up and down the street. Halloween was more about candy than costumes. We would run as fast as we could from house to house, gathering as much candy as possible. Many people gave apples instead of candy, which was always a disappointment. Our refrain at the door was, "Halloween apples". I always wondered if that was the reason we got so many. Apples were heavy and weighed down the pillowcase we used for collecting our goodies. Mom always made apple pies out of the bruised and battered apples we dragged home, so they weren't a complete waste.

Every house on our street but one handed out Halloween treats. Mr. Blackmore lived at the far end of Newman Street and was the only neighbor that did not take part. Surrounding Mr. Blackmore's house was a neatly trimmed, six-foot hedge. The only way into his yard was through a tall gate which he always locked. I know he locked it because we tried to open it every Halloween. I don't know why Mr. Blackmore did not want kids coming to his door, but we came up with several ideas and had great fun making up ghastly tales about his dislike of children. If Mr. Blackmore didn't like us, then we didn't like him. That is why we conspired to scare him out of his wits.

It was a few days past Halloween but Kenny and I were still in a spooky frame of mind and decided to create some tiny ghosts. From my house, we collected white rags, scissors, string, tape, and a black felt marker. We searched Kenny's garage and found the perfect sticks. After filling the white rags with leaves, we tied the bottoms with string. We inserted a stick into each one and drew menacing black eyes on the white cloth. Our collection of creepy little ghosts had come together nicely, and our hard work had paid off. To our young minds these little rag ghosts looked absolutely real, and we were certain it would scare Mr. Blackmore out of his pants.

We snuck up to his front yard and placed ten little ghosts along the top of his tall hedge. When Mr. Blackmore exited his front door, they would be there to greet him, and scare the daylights out of him. We worked fast, hoping he wouldn't come out before we finished. As soon as we were done, we ran to the other end of the street and hid under the branches of a big spruce tree. We were eager to see Mr. Blackmore's reaction, but did not dare go anywhere near his house for the rest of the day.

The following day Kenny and I wandered past Mr. Blackmore's house to check it out. All the ghosts had disappeared from the top of his hedge. We were certain Mr. Blackmore was still inside, shaking like a leaf... too afraid to step outside his door ever again...

Kool-Aid for Sale

It was a sizzling hot summer day and my friend Margo asked if I wanted to help her set up a Kool-Aid stand. We made a huge jug of cherry Kool-Aid, and scribbled a sign on a piece of cardboard, "Ice Cold Kool-Aid". We borrowed a few glasses from her mom's cupboard, and a small camping table from her basement. Off we went to make our fortune.

The bus stop outside Dominion Drugstore seemed the ideal spot to set up shop. We prepared the little table with cups and Kool-Aid and propped up the scribbled sign. All we had to do now was wait for people to show up. It seemed like an eternity before a man and a woman wandered up to the bus stop. Margo asked if they would like a cup of ice-cold Kool-Aid while they waited for the bus. They did, so she poured them two big glassfuls. The man took a sip, made a face, and handed it back. "This Kool-Aid is hot", he shouted! Margo could not find ice in her freezer when we made the Kool-Aid, and the jug had been sitting in the hot sun for quite some time. The woman also handed hers back. Margo reached out to return their money, when the bus pulled up. The couple hopped on the bus, leaving the money behind. Nobody would want warm Kool-Aid, but where were we going to get ice?

The money was burning a hole in Margo's pocket so she wanted to buy popsicles. We left our table and ran into Dominion Drug

Store. They kept the ice cream and popsicles in a huge freezer chest with a glass lid. The freezer walls were always covered in thick white frost, which broke off if you jiggled it. Margo saw this as the answer to our ice problem. The popsicles would have to wait. Margo and I set to jiggling and pulling off hunks of the frost. With our arms full of thick white frost, we hurried out of the store and back to our table. We plopped the slabs of frost into the jug of Kool-Aid. It now looked ice cold, just as our sign advertised.

This however, was short lived. With the hot sun beating down, the frost melted in no time. No one seemed interested in buying from us anyway so we closed up shop. Margo didn't want to carry the full jug of Kool-Aid home and decided to drink it. We filled two glasses to the top and took a big mouthful. Yuck! It was horrible! Freezer frost is gross and tastes nothing like ice. Good thing nobody bought any…

The Claw Game

Mom occasionally sent me to my room as a punishment for misbehaving. I am not sure what I had done on this day to warrant such discipline, but she ordered me to my room, and told me not to come out until she called.

I sat on my bed for what seemed like an eternity waiting for my mom to tell me I could come out. There was nothing interesting to do, and I was bored to death. My room was on the second floor with one window that opened easily. I opened the window and hung my head out to check on what was happening outside. My window faced the back lane so there wasn't much to see. The back porch was below my window and I noticed there was a lot of interesting stuff sitting on it. As I studied the objects on the porch, it reminded me of the claw game at Winnipeg Beach Amusement Park. In this game you would maneuver a mechanical claw to pick up one of the many toys in the glass case. It was almost impossible to grab one of the good prizes, but you could sometimes snag one of the cheap ones that nobody wanted. It was not long before inspiration struck, and I was inventing my own version of the claw game from my window.

I would need something long to reach down to the porch below. I scanned my room to see what I could use. My housecoat was on the chair so I removed the belt from it. I then tied a plastic belt from my new pedal pushers to that. I could find nothing else that was long and rope like, so I tied the arms of two sweaters together and attached that to my makeshift rope. It still wasn't long enough, so I tied the sleeves of my school blouse to all of this and pulled it tight. I then secured a wire coat hanger to the end for a hook and checked to see if it would reach the porch. It did not go quite far enough, but if I leaned out the window I could make it reach. A shovel was resting upright below my window and I tried for it first. This was the same shovel I had gotten my tongue stuck on last winter. There were some unpleasant memories linked to this shovel.

I dropped my makeshift rope out the window and snagged the handle of the shovel on the first try. It banged against the wall as I lifted it up. I pulled it through the window and into my room. The next object I retrieved was a black and red metal bucket. This was trickier because the handle was small and hard to grasp. After a few tries I was able to maneuver it on to the coat hanger and pull it up and into my room. I then captured an empty wooden apple box and added it to my collection. I was deciding on what to hook next when my mother barged into my room. She spotted the junk pile at my feet, and me hanging halfway out the window, and demanded to know what on earth I was doing?

The kitchen window was right below my bedroom. Mom was in the kitchen visiting with one of her friends when she noticed strange objects going up past the window. Mom assumed it involved me and came upstairs to investigate. She told me in no uncertain terms I was not to be hanging out the window, or dragging things into my room. I had to spend twice as long in my room for punishment.

I am certain I could have grabbed everything on the porch if mom hadn't put a stop to my fun...

Horses and Folks that Visited Our Street

The days of horse and buggy had long departed Winnipeg streets, but the odd horse pulled wagon would occasionally make its way down Newman Street, creating quite a stir amongst us kids. It was thrilling to see a horse in the city, on our very own street. The hooves of the horse would make a loud, clippity-clop, clatter on the road. We would run alongside and pester the driver to, "Give us a ride!" The old guys driving the wagons were all grouches and ignored us. We kept on asking anyway. One crabby guy selling cow manure, or "lawn dressing" as the sign politely read, came down our street every spring with a wagon heaped full of stinky brown stuff that smelled awful! We did not want a ride on his wagon. We would just follow that guy to the end of the street and chat to his horse. Another old man came down our street every fall with an enormous load of fresh vegetables for sale. Most of the moms would come out and buy things from him. His bony old horse was at least a hundred years old and wore blinders and a canvas bag over his mouth. I felt sad for that horse, trudging down our street and pulling that heavy load. Another wagon overflowing with rusty old junk metal sometimes visited our street. I don't know if that guy sold the junk, or collected it along the way.

A few homes on our street still had iceboxes instead of electric refrigerators. An ice truck brought huge blocks of ice to those houses. The kids would always escort the ice truck down the street because hunks of ice would break off when the man grabbed the huge ice blocks with his sharp tongs. That chunk of cold, clean ice, tasted as good as any popsicle, and it was free!

A coal truck came every week to deliver coal to the houses that used it. There was a coal chute at the side of our house and the coal man would empty bags of coal into it. You could not miss the coal man's arrival if you were inside the house. The coal made a huge racket as it tumbled down the coal chute to the basement.

Another regular visitor to our street and house, was the Eaton's deliveryman. Eaton's Department Store used to do home deliveries. It was always the same friendly delivery guy. He was very comfortable with all his customers and never waited for an invitation to come into their homes. He would knock on the door, walk right in, and yell. "Eaton's!" I don't think my shy, extremely private mother, appreciated him barging into our home as he did. She was too nice to say anything though.

The Avon lady would regularly show up at our door as would the Watkins man. Mom bought things from both. From Avon she would buy a yellow hand cream in a green jar. I loved the smell of that cream. It was a scent I would remember and associate with my mother many, many years later. From the Watkins man mom would buy black pepper, vanilla, and an ointment that smelled like Vicks. Once a year, an odd-looking man showed up at our door and would hand my mom a card that said he was a deaf-mute. He would then hold up a small sewing kit for her to buy. Even though mom owned a huge sewing kit with more needles and thread than she could use in a lifetime, she always purchased the man's small kit. After the door shut, mom always said the same thing, "I do not believe that man is a deaf-mute". I suspect she gave him the benefit of the doubt, and bought his needles and thread, just in case. Mom was fond of reciting little ditties, and one of them was… "It's better to trust all and be deceived, then to doubt one fond heart that should be believed". I am pretty certain that pertained to the deaf-mute guy…

The Dinner Table

My British mother insisted on proper table manners and often reminded her children, "They were not being raised in a barn!" We ate at the kitchen table six days of the week, but on Sundays we enjoyed roast beef dinners in the dining room, where even stricter rules applied. Proper etiquette demanded there be no elbows on the table, asking for dishes to be passed instead of reaching, no talking with your mouth full, using a knife instead of your finger to push food onto your fork, waiting for everyone to sit before eating, asking to be excused if you needed to leave the table, and not leaving the table until everyone else finished eating. They always broke this last rule on the days we had turnip. Mom was a wonderful cook, and I liked most everything that came out of her kitchen… except for turnip. There was nothing she could do to turnip to make me like it. It made me gag, and I refused to swallow it. Mom seemed to think my health, and entire wellbeing, depended on me getting turnip into my body. She took a firm stand on this, and would not allow me to leave the table until I finished my turnip. I would eat everything else on my plate, but not the dreaded orange lump that remained. Everyone at the table would tire of waiting for me to finish, and would leave one by one. I would be left all alone, creating pretty designs in the mushy turnip with my fork. When a sufficient amount of time passed, I would stuff the turnip into my pocket, or my napkin. Sometimes I would resort to a little trick I picked up from my seven hamsters and would pack the turnip into my cheeks so I could spit it out later. I don't think mom was the slightest bit fooled by my "disappearing turnip tricks". I suspect she became weary of my little games. It never stopped her from trying again the next time though.

There was a time during my childhood I spilled my glass of milk at every meal. Mom always laid a crisp, pressed cloth on the table at mealtimes and was not thrilled with me soaking it in milk every day. My sisters, Eileen and Rose, got a kick out of me spilling my milk, and waited in eager anticipation for it to happen. The harder I tried not to spill, the more often I did, so mom came up with a plan. She cut a huge piece of plastic into a square and placed it right where I sat, which solved the problem. That piece of plastic remained at my spot for much longer than necessary. I wasn't even spilling any longer. Eileen and Rose loved that I still had the plastic and thought it funny. To my way of thinking, that alone was reason enough to keep it.

I passed through a phase where I was a bit of a Germaphobe. I did not have the slightest problem getting my hands dirty while handling mud, worms, frogs or other distasteful things, and I was not the slightest bit bothered by dogs licking my face, but I had a severe aversion to people sharing my drinks or food. My sisters and I were always good at sharing with each other and were glad to do so. I would share everything of mine, except for a few things. Excluded from my sharing list were, ice cream cones, popsicles, candy apples, suckers and drinks of any kind. Instead of allowing them to lick my ice cream or sip my drink, I would make them wait until I was halfway through, and then give them the rest. They didn't seem to mind my germs and welcomed whatever I was willing to share. At the dinner table my sisters loved to tease me by lifting my glass of milk and pretending to drink from it. This would spark an outburst from me, "Put my milk down, if you put your mouth on it I won't drink it!" My sisters loved this game. They also enjoyed another stunt which they pulled on me many times. If for any reason I had to leave the table, even for a second, I would return to find my sisters smirking and staring at my glass of milk. Upon careful inspection of my milk glass, I would notice the milk had been sloshed around, as if someone had taken a sip. With Eileen and Rose sitting there smiling, I would demand to know who had taken a sip from my glass. Because I would refuse to finish my milk, mom would intervene, "Don't do that to her!" Mom would try to convince me that no one had put their mouth on my glass. She would explain that one of my sisters had picked up the glass and swirled the milk around to make it look as if someone had taken a sip. I always believed what mom told me, but I did not trust the smirks on my sisters faces. No way was I going to drink that milk...

God, Save the Queen

Mom and dad had British roots and a proud British heritage. They were staunch supporters and ardent lovers of all things British. They spoke about their much-loved country of England often. Dad's family was from London and my mom was born in Yorkshire, England.

It was always time for tea at our house, and they always served it hot and in a proper teacup, along with a homemade cookie or scone. In the winter our breakfast always included a hot cup of tea to warm us up before the walk through the snow to school.

My parents adored the Royal family and discussed in great detail any bit of news concerning the Royal Palace, the Queen mother, Queen Elizabeth, and her entire household. Mom and dad were on a first name basis with all. They referred to the Queen as Elizabeth. We knew the Queen's husband, the Duke of Edinburgh, as Phillip; although they sometimes referred to him as the scallywag. I'm not sure what that was all about. Their four kids, Charles the Prince of Wales, Anne the Princess Royal, Prince Andrew the Duke of York, and Prince Edward the Earl of Wessex, were fondly referred to as the Queens' children. We were chummy with them all. Countless conversations between my parents or my grandparents started with, "Have you heard what our Phillip's been up to?" or "Did you see what they wrote about Elizabeth?" We heard about the Queen and her family so frequently, and in so much detail, I assumed they were somehow related to us. Over time, I became convinced of it, which is why I began casually mentioning it to the kids at school. Everyone at school was familiar with the Queen, because Canada's flag at the time was the Union Jack, and we started every school day singing, "God Save the Queen", followed by "O Canada", a Hymn, and the Lord's Prayer.

Most of the kids didn't think much of it when I told them I was related to the Royal family. There were some however that didn't believe me and did not hesitate to let me know. When I told my mom that kids at school were making fun of me because they didn't believe we were related to the Queen, she looked horrified. "Why on earth are you spreading such malarkey? I hope to goodness you did not tell your teacher that!" When I told her I may have mentioned it to my teacher, she shook her head and sighed.

I was wrong about our family's Royal connection, and mom made it exceedingly clear. We are not related to the Queen, or to anyone in the Royal family, and I was to stop spreading such rubbish!

Well, this was embarrassing, and rather disappointing. The Queen seemed like quite a nice lady. She clearly would not be popping into our home for tea any time soon...

You are Filthy

I had to have ten times as many baths as my sister. Rose always looked immaculate while I didn't stay clean for any time at all. When I came in from playing, mom would take one look at me and holler, "You are filthy! What have you been doing?" I honestly did not know how I got so dirty. I never paid much attention to dirt when I was playing. My clothes got filthy and my little body underneath did too.

Mom would march me up the stairs, fill the bathtub with steaming hot soapy water and order me in. She would scrub and scour me like I was one of her dirty kitchen pots. The water in the tub would be murky after she finished with me. When I was clean enough for her liking, she would dry me off and dress me in clean, freshly ironed clothes, underpants and all. Mom could never figure out how one little girl could get so dirty. Dirt and fun went hand in hand as far as I was concerned.

Rose, who wasn't even dirty, would sometimes climb in the tub with me just for fun. Our bathtub was a whopping big, cast iron thing with claw feet. Ten kids could fit in that tub! We had so much fun in that big tub and were never in a rush to get out. When we did finish, we would drain the water out and rub soap all over ourselves and all over the inside of the tub. We would slide down the sloped back and slip and slither round and round, flying up the sides, and down again. This was definitely the very best part about taking a bath...

Our Kitchen

Our comfy little home on Newman Street had three-bedrooms, one-bathroom, a living room, dining room, and a large kitchen. The kitchen was the hub of our home, and it was there that the most interesting things happened. One large bright light on the ceiling lit up the entire kitchen. You might have your hair cut with special hair trimming scissors, or curled with a smoking hot curling iron while sitting on a chair under that light. Slivers were removed from hands with a sewing needle, and countless cuts and scrapes were cleaned up and bandaged. Crayons or other foreign objects were retrieved from noses, and heads were examined for cuts, lumps and bruises after crashes. My sister had her ears pierced by our Auntie Rosa under that light. She did this using a darning needle, heavy black thread, ice cubes and a bar of soap. Rose was as pale as a ghost and visibly shaking. It was difficult to watch, and I felt terrible for my sister. She must have really wanted those ears pierced, because she did not chicken out, even though she could have. Other than the nervous shaking, she stayed surprisingly still.

I once jammed a giant, red and white, plastic whistle so far into my mouth it got wedged. Dad put me in the chair under the kitchen light and had me lean back. He pulled and twisted the whistle, but it would not budge. Resolving issues was one of his specialties, but this one puzzled him. Mom fretted, and offered many suggestions, but nothing helped. Dad went to his toolbox and returned with a pair of pliers. I was positive there wasn't room in my mouth for both the whistle and those pliers. Dad gripped the whistle with the pliers and gave a tug, but it hurt so much he had to stop. Moving on to Plan B, he squeezed the pliers with enough force to snap the whistle in two with a loud crack! Out popped the whistle. Mom breathed a huge sigh of relief.

Dad reminded me of the day I had stuffed fourteen marshmallows into that mouth. This incredible feat took place at the cottage when my aunts were visiting. We were all sitting around the big table when someone wondered how many marshmallows a person could fit into their mouth at one time. People had differing opinions on the subject, so we had a contest to see who could put in the most. Auntie Rosa brought the marshmallows over to the table, and the challenge began. Everyone put marshmallows into their mouths, one at a time. There was considerable laughter and carrying on as marshmallow after marshmallow was added. Mom, not being a huge competitor, stopped at one. My dad, aunts and sisters stopped somewhere around seven. With everybody cheering me on, there was no way I was stopping. My cheeks were puffed out like a chipmunk and I could not close my mouth. No one caught on to the fact the marshmallows in the back of my mouth were melting, and I was swallowing most of them. I would swallow one and replace it with another. I could have gone on like that forever, except I was becoming a little queasy from all the sugar and quit at fourteen. I held the title of "marshmallow mouth stuffing champion" for years to come…

Wolves and a Miracle Medicine

We had three bedrooms in our house. Mom and dad slept in one, Granny Brooks, who lived with us for part of my childhood, slept in another, and Eileen, Rose, and I shared the third bedroom and one bed. It was fun sleeping together but Eileen was not thrilled when one of us younger girls wet the bed and climbed on top of her to get away from the wet part.

I was certain wolves lived under our bed and was reluctant to step down onto the floor. Not only did wolves live under our bed, they also hung out in the bathroom. When Rose or I had to go to the bathroom at night, we would never go alone. We would wake each other and make the trip together. Rose had a serious kidney problem that caused her to have to go to the bathroom a lot. The doctor didn't know how to treat her kidney trouble, so we made frequent night-time bathroom trips.

These trips became less frequent after a surprise phone call from our family doctor. He had heard about a new medication that could help Rose with her kidney problem and phoned to let my parents know. Mom and dad immediately made an appointment to discuss it with him. The doctor told them the medication was very costly and may prohibit them from getting it. Mom said his exact words were, "It will be like swallowing gold." Dad told the doctor he would get a second mortgage on our house if needed, and Rose would have the medication.

I don't know if they re-mortgaged our house or not, but I know they sold the piano about that time. Mom and dad both played piano and Eileen and Rose were taking piano lessons. My parents were always good at setting their priorities, and their children were at the top of that list.

Everyone was thankful when the medication worked and Rose's kidney problem improved. Rose and I had to make a lot fewer night-time trips to the bathroom after that. Those rotten wolves got lonely and left...

Risky Games and a Row of Black Stitches

Several games Rose and I played always ended with one of us getting hurt. One activity that never ended well was tobogganing down the stairs on a piece of cardboard. It took some persuading to get Rose to join me as she thought it was too dangerous. It always surprised me at how fast we could go! We would fly down the stairs, causing the metal rods that held the carpet in place to come loose and airborne. The wall was close to the bottom of the stairs, which often made for a painful landing. Mom was not a big fan of this activity and was never happy about having to put the metal rods back into their little holes.

Our favorite game was jumping on the bed together with a blanket over our heads. That just about always ended in disaster. We would end up clunking our heads together or nosediving off the bed onto the hardwood floor. It hurt, but didn't stop us from getting back up and doing it again.

We were doing triple flips on the bed when I missed and smacked my head on the edge of the sharp metal headboard. My forehead split wide open! With blood gushing and my hand over my forehead, I ran to show mom. She was having a bath and had locked the bathroom door. I banged and shouted, "Mom, come out and see something!" She responded, "I will look when

I am finished having my bath." I knocked louder and yelled, "You need to come and look right now!" That got her attention. She opened the bathroom door and stood there in her robe, eager to know what was so important. I removed my hand with a bit of a flourish. "Oh no, what did you do!" It must have looked bad because my mom called dad at work and told him he would have to come home and take me to the hospital. Our family never went to the hospital.

Dad rushed home and off we went. The trip to Emergency did not take long at all. The nurse looked at my head and ushered us to the back. A young doctor examined my split forehead and said I would need stitches to close it up. He told us we would have to wait for the senior doctor who would not be available for a while. "Oh, it's not very hard to stitch up a gash," said dad. "If you bring me the needle and thread, I will do it." I don't know if dad was kidding, but the young doctor laughed. He said he could not let dad do it, but he would give it a go if my dad didn't mind. Give it a go? I did not like the sound of that, but dad agreed and it was apparently settled. The doctor draped a blue cloth over my eyes so I couldn't see what was happening. It hurt when the needle went in, and I could feel him pulling the thread through, but it was not so bad. He was done in no time.

Dad had to get back to work, but found time to make a quick stop at Dominion Drugstore so I could pick a treat for being so good. I chose a chocolate ice cream cone. Getting stitches wasn't such a bad thing after all. I could hardly wait to get home and show the kids on the street my cool stitched up head...

I Did Love Rings

Another time mom called dad home from work was when I forced a small curtain ring onto my finger. I was obsessed with rings and often put anything and everything resembling a ring on my fingers. A small curtain ring had fallen off the rod above the kitchen sink and I could not resist trying it on my finger. It was a bit small, so I pushed hard, forcing it past my knuckle. I held my hand up, admiring it and thinking it looked quite nice. It wasn't long before my finger began to hurt. I tried to pull the curtain ring off but it wouldn't budge. My swollen finger was turning red and nothing I did helped. When my finger changed from red to blue, I hurried to show my mom. She panicked, certain my finger would fall off if she did not do something fast. Mom felt she had no choice but to call dad at work. Dad must have driven fast because he was home before I knew it. I was glad to see him. He took one look at my blue, swollen finger and said he would try to cut it off. I hoped he was talking about the curtain ring, not my finger.

A chair was placed under the bright kitchen light, and I took a seat. Dad dug through his toolbox and decided on several small files and a tiny saw. He tried the file first, sawing back and forth through the metal. The sawing made the metal hot, which made my finger hurt more, so he sawed slower. It was working, and he was making excellent progress. When he got close to the skin, he stopped sawing and separated the cut metal with a screwdriver and some small pliers. My dark blue finger turned a healthy pink and felt much better with the blood flowing. After a little more prying and pulling, the curtain ring slipped off my finger. Mom breathed a huge sigh of relief. I thanked dad and promised I would not put anything on my finger that wasn't an actual ring ever again, and I meant it...

The Exquisite Gold Heart Ring

I won a real ring as a prize at a birthday party. It was gold with two small hearts. It was beautiful, and I loved it. I pushed it onto my finger and planned on never taking it off for the rest of my life. It was so much nicer than the curtain rings, washers, bolts, elastics, and other ring-shaped doodads I'd previously forced onto my fingers. I had stopped doing that after the curtain ring disaster, as I didn't like rings anymore. However, this beautiful gold ring with the two little hearts made me fall in love with rings all over again. It fit and looked fabulous on my little hand.

My joy however was short lived. Rings seemed to always get me into trouble. I was watching TV. I must have been absorbed in the show because I didn't realize I was gnawing on the gold ring causing it to kink and press into my finger at several spots. My first clue something was wrong was that my finger hurt. I tried to pull the ring off, but it would not budge. I kept tugging, which hurt even more. My finger puffed up, turning red and then dark blue, just as it had when I'd jammed that curtain ring on. I hurried to the kitchen to show my mom. She took a quick look and shouted, "Oh no, not again!" My granny was visiting and also had a look. Granny came up with a lot of good ideas and they tried them all. They smeared butter on my finger, soaked my hand in ice water, and pulled and pried with pliers, to no avail. My finger was blue, ugly, throbbing, and getting worse. Granny suggested mom call a taxi and take me to the Emergency Room at the Hospital.

A yellow taxi pulled up to our house, and granny, mom, and I piled into the back seat. My family never called taxicabs, so this was a brand-new experience. If my finger wasn't hurting so much I would have quite enjoyed it. We arrived at the Emergency room and went up to the counter. I could tell it was killing mom to explain why were there, but the nurse didn't act like this was the first ring disaster to have come through the door. She ushered mom and me to the back, where we sat waiting for the doctor. The doctor appeared and studied my swollen, blue, throbbing finger. It seemed he was trying to figure out how to get it off. I was just about to tell him he should call and ask my dad, when he jumped up and announced he would be right back. He returned with a thing that looked like a tiny can opener. He slid this under my crumpled ring and cut in two places. It fell right off. He examined my finger which was now a healthy pink and determined there was no actual harm done. We were free to go. Mom thanked him profusely. The doctor handed me the two halves of my once beautiful gold heart ring. Rings are quite dangerous and get stuck for hardly any reason at all...

Every Man His Own Doctor

It was a rare occasion when any of us went to an actual doctor or hospital. My parents, grandparents, and perhaps their grandparents before them, understood all there was to know about curing and treating just about any ailment known to man. They gleaned much of this knowledge from experience, and some of it from two old books I once found while rummaging through a cupboard at the cottage. The books were entitled, "The Family Physician-every man his own Doctor", written in 1905 and "Enquire Within Upon Everything" written in 1900. These books were ancient. My grandparents must have passed all this valuable knowledge down to my parents, because they used a lot of those remedies on us kids.

The two most popular germ killers used in our home were Iodine and Mercurochrome. If you cut yourself for any reason, or scraped the skin off your knee or elbow, they would treat the wound with one of these. The Iodine came in a small bottle with a rubber stopper and a smooth glass applicator. I liked the Mercurochrome better because it stung less than the Iodine and stained your skin a brilliant reddish orange color. If your gashes were especially dirty, they would pour peroxide on first. I loved watching it fizz and bubble.

I once jumped off of a fence onto a board that had a long rusty nail sticking out. I didn't see the nail because it was covered in horse dung. My brand-new runners had thin soles and did not prevent the nail from going straight through and deep into my foot. It hurt like heck! I pulled my foot from the manure-covered nail and removed my shoe and bloody sock. I could see the hole in my foot where the nail had penetrated it. I was most upset about the hole in my new runner and the yucky brown stuff that stained the white canvas. It was later in the evening that my foot really started to hurt. The skin was hot and red around the puncture site. I showed my parents and told them about the manure-covered nail that had pierced it. Mom cleansed the wound and soaked my foot in hot water. She made a poultice out of bread and warm water and placed it on my foot. This was covered in plastic and a small towel and held together with one of dad's large socks. Mom changed the bread poultice several times a day and kept a close eye on the wound. After a few days, the redness was gone and my foot looked good.

Another home remedy was mom's famous mustard plaster. For the flu, colds, coughs and pneumonia, mom would concoct a mixture of dry mustard and warm water and sprinkle it onto a warm cloth, covered by more cloths. She placed this on your chest or back. It smelled terrible and burned if any of it leaked out of the cloth. I think I preferred the cough to the mustard plaster.

There was a bottle of medicinal brandy on the top shelf of the kitchen cupboard. A dash of brandy was mixed with warm water, honey and lemon to help you sleep when you had a bad cold. It tasted horrible. For earaches, mom would get out her glass ear syringe and put some warm drops of oil into our ears. She would then stuff each ear with a piece of cotton. Sometimes we would go to school with cotton stuffed in our ears. Mom also had a glass eye cup she used if you had an eye infection. I don't know what she put into this perfect little eye shaped glass cup but it stung a bit. We had to place the tiny cup over our open eye and tip the liquid in. It was messy and fun to do. For poison ivy, chicken pox, rashes and itchy skin, calamine lotion would be in order. There was an outbreak of impetigo at our school and kids were getting it on their bottoms, from sitting on the school toilet seats. Mom was a firm believer that toilet seats were the grimiest things in the world. That is why she always insisted we squat instead of sit, on every toilet seat outside of our home. Rose and I must have been living on the edge and not heeding mom's advice, because we both got impetigo on our bottoms at the same time. The treatment for impetigo was gentian violet. This bright purple liquid was more permanent than the best indelible ink in the world. It turned your skin a brilliant purple and would not wash off, even after several baths. We had purple stained bottoms and several pairs of purple stained underpants for quite some time. It was great stuff!

Mom treated stomach aches or leg aches with an Aspirin and a well-used red rubber hot water bottle. She filled the hot water bottle with steaming water from the kettle which gave it a rubbery smell. She then wrapped a soft towel around it. That old hot water bottle with its distinct, familiar smell, had magical powers. It almost always made me feel better. Mom was skillful at nursing us and overseeing our health and wellness. We didn't just survive; we thrived under her excellent care...

"Spit Girl"

I assume there was nothing in the Home Cures book about dental procedures because we went to an actual dentist for our teeth. His name was Dr. Toe. I always thought Dr. Tooth would have been a better name for a dentist.

Dr. Toe's office was in an old house that had been made into a dental office. Gwen was his assistant and his receptionist. My parents never allowed us to call adults by their first names but Gwen always insisted we do. The office was close to our home so Rose and I would walk there together. We didn't mind going for check-ups, but hated to have a filling. It hurt a lot whenever Dr. Toe did any work on our teeth and he terrified us. If Rose and I both needed a filling on the same day, Dr. Toe would come out to the tiny waiting room and ask, "Which one gets to go first?" Did he think we would fight over who got to go first? If we had to go at all, we preferred to go last, not first. The conversation between Rose and me went something like this, "You go first." "No, you go first." "I'm not going, you go." Dr. Toe would become impatient and choose one of us at random. If Rose was the one that went in first for a filling, I would sit in the waiting room worrying and feeling badly the whole time. I felt just as glad when Rose finished as I did when it was me.

I don't think Dr. Toe had the most modern equipment in the world. He had a very slow drill, a wire thing that wiggled and shook as it went around. When Dr. Toe drilled your tooth, your whole head vibrated! He never once offered to give us freezing. He claimed it would be quicker and would save our dad some money if he drilled without it. He didn't know our dad well. Dad would have spent the extra dollar on some freezing if he knew how much Dr. Toe was torturing us. Dr. Toe always made a point of mentioning how well-behaved Rose and I were. He said most youngsters didn't sit as still as we did. I don't think it was because we were so well-behaved that we remained so still; we were afraid to move in case the drill slipped and went straight through our cheeks! We knew the torture was over when we heard him say, "Spit girl"! Once you spit into the teeny, round, white sink beside the dental chair, the pain and torment was over, and you were free to go.

When we were both done Dr. Toe would walk with us to the door, smile big, showing his perfect white dentist teeth, and say, "Don't forget to brush!" We would give him a half-hearted little wave and get the heck out of there as quick as we could…

My Sisters were Good at Sharing

My sisters and I were always good at sharing things with each other, but Rose was the best sharer in the world. Rose seemed to love sharing, and would share absolutely everything. I loved candy, and it was impossible for me to save my Halloween candy, Easter treats, or Christmas goodies for even two days. I would try to spread it out and make it last longer, but it just wasn't possible. I firmly believed candy was for eating not saving. Rose ate just a little of her candy every day, making it last for weeks. Because mine was all gone, she would feel badly and offer to share hers. I always felt guilty taking advantage of her generous nature, but I did love candy. Rose was also better at saving money. To pass the time, we would sometimes count how much money we each had. We would bring out our stockpile of coins we had been saving and sit on the floor to compare. Rose always had a lot more than I did. I don't know where my money went, but I always had less. Because Rose did not like to see me with less, she would suggest we put our money together and divide it. She hated to have more of anything and always wanted me to have the same amount. It never mattered to her I had squandered what I had, or made a pig of myself eating all my treats at once. She insisted we put it all together, divide it, and start again with an equal amount. The weird thing about it was, Rose seemed to genuinely enjoy doing this. It's who she was, and what made her so special.

Eileen was also great at sharing. This worked out nicely for Rose and me. Eileen was eight years older than me, and six and a half years older than Rose. Eileen worked at Eaton's Department store and must have spent a big chunk of her paycheck on clothes, because she had a lot of them. Dad had to build an addition to the closet in our room, to store the extra clothes. Mohair sweaters were in style and Eileen had one of every style and color. Rose and I could borrow them whenever we wanted and Eileen never once complained. Rose and I began to look quite stylish with Eileen working and expanding her wardrobe.

We thought Eileen was sophisticated and beautiful. Eileen was the shortest of us three girls at just under five feet, which is probably why she wore spike heels everywhere she went. She even wore high heels with blue jeans. It always amazed me how fast she could walk in those spike heels. Eileen wore her hair in a fashionable beehive and changed her hair color regularly. We never knew what color her hair would be on her return from the hairdresser. She went from blond, to white, to grey, to black, to brown, and one time pink. I think the pink may have been a hairdressing mishap as it didn't stay that color long. When Eileen married and left home, Rose and I were sad to see her go. We would miss our older sister, and would certainly miss all those clothes she let us borrow…

Sandy Hook Summers

As kids we spent our summers at Sandy Hook. Sandy Hook sits between Winnipeg Beach and the town of Gimli on Lake Winnipeg. Dad and his father built a little cottage on the lake front, many years before I was even born. We would go to the lake as soon as school was out and stay until school started again in the fall. I loved the cottage, and I loved the freedom. We lived in our bathing suits and ran barefoot all summer. We roasted countless hotdogs and marshmallows over roaring bonfires and ate bowls of fresh raspberries covered in fresh cream purchased from the farm down the road. We enjoyed delicious fresh pickerel, drank Kool-Aid by the gallon, and popped popcorn in the fireplace.

Sandy Hook was my favorite place on earth. I have so many fond memories of summers spent in that cozy little cabin. Many aunts, uncles and cousins visited, and there was always lots of joking, laughter and kind-hearted teasing. The beautiful stone fireplace my father built, was the focal point of the cabin, and it was there everyone gathered. The rocks that went into the fireplace were hauled up from the beach one by one. Every time the adults came back from swimming out front, they carried a rock with them and added it to the pile. When there were enough rocks, my dad, who was a gifted stone mason, built the fireplace. Some of my best childhood memories are associated with sitting around that fireplace in the evening in front of a roaring fire. Dad would sometimes play his accordion, harmonica or ukulele, or we would play games. Dad would often wind up the old gramophone and put a 78 RPM record on to play. He had a great collection of records and one of our favorites was "Barney Google, With the Goo Goo Googly Eyes". Us kids loved that one and would sing along to the scratchy, tinny sounding tune. Our absolute favorite record, was the "laughing record". As the title suggests, it was a record of people laughing. The laughter would build until someone on the record laughed so hard they would snort. Every time dad played that record us kids would swear we weren't going to giggle, but we could only hold it in until the lady on the record snorted. As soon as that happened we would burst out laughing, and continue howling until the record finished. It was impossible not to laugh, no matter how hard you tried.

Dad and his sisters loved teasing and playing jokes on each other and us kids. For as long as I can remember there was an authentic looking fried egg made of rubber, and a realistic-looking rubber wiener hidden in the back of the cupboard. Guests or visitors to the cabin were certain to be served the egg or wiener during their stay. Dad, or one of my aunts, would cook bacon, fried eggs and toast for breakfast and give the rubber egg to the unsuspecting visitor. They took great care to make it look the same as the real fried egg sitting beside it on the plate. The two eggs were arranged side by side and bacon grease was drizzled on top of both. They added bacon and cut toast to the plate before they put it in front of the unsuspecting guest. Us kids would hold our breath and wait for the victim to take the first bite. When they couldn't figure out why they weren't able to cut the rubber egg, we would roar with laughter. The person being fooled would laugh even harder.

The rubber hotdog prank was pretty much the same as the rubber egg trick. They put the rubber wiener into a real hotdog bun with relish, mustard, cheese and onions and wait for the unwary guest to take the first bite. When the guest could not bite through the wiener, the giggles would start. You didn't have to be a guest to get the rubber egg or rubber hotdog. Sometimes my dad, or one of my aunts, would sneak one of these onto one of our plates. That was every bit as funny, and we always fell for it.

The rubber wiener had a dual purpose when Auntie Rosa visited. The old clock on the mantel chimed every hour, day and night. Auntie Rosa could not sleep because of the chiming, and would stuff the rubber hotdog between the bell and the clanger to silence the clock.

Our cabin had no plumbing or running water, and in the very early years we did not have electricity. We used coal oil lamps and an old wood-burning stove to do all the cooking. The fire in the stove was lit first thing every morning, and the kettle was filled with water from a bucket and heated for washing and tea. Mom would cook the most delicious bacon, eggs and waffles on that stove. The toaster was a four-sided, open wire contraption, which sat over the open flame. When one side of the bread was toasted, you had to flip it over so the other side could toast. This was harder than it looked, and more times than not the toast was burnt. No one complained or minded. Scraping the burnt part off with your knife was just something you did when you were at the lake.

After breakfast, us girls would brush our teeth outdoors. We would take our toothbrushes, toothpaste and a small glass of water to dunk our brushes in. We would stand outside and spit toothpaste water into the bushes. It was much more fun than brushing your teeth in the city with a sink and running water. We would then get a basin and fill it with warm water from the stove so we could wash our hands and faces.

There were always three buckets of water by the stove. One was from the rain barrel, and two came from the pump. The pump was a short walk down the lane and had its own little wooden house. Going to the pump for water was something my sisters and I would often do. Taking the wagon and two empty buckets, we would head off down the gravel road to the pump house. We would place the bucket under the spout and pump like crazy until the water flowed, filling the buckets to the top with icy water from the artesian well. We would pull the wagon back home along the bumpy gravel road, splashing water all the way. By the time we arrived home, our full buckets would be half empty. The third bucket of water by the stove was for washing and came from the rain barrel outside the door. When you got water from the rain barrel, you always banged the metal dipper on the side before dipping. There were always several mosquito larvae swimming around the top of the water and banging with the dipper caused the larvae to swim to the bottom of the barrel, leaving the water at the top clear and larvae free. The rain water bucket sat right beside the clean drinking water buckets, and we were always careful not to mix the buckets up. Nobody wanted to drink the water from the rain barrel by mistake...

The Outhouse, Spiders, and an Old Shed

Because we had no plumbing at the lake, we had to use the outhouse at the back of our property. Mom was always very meticulous. She cleaned and scrubbed the outhouse every day, but it was impossible to keep it free from spiders. The spiders at the lake were not like the ones you see in your basement in the city. These spiders were monstrous! Some of them had bodies the size of grapes, with long and hairy legs. The spiders seemed to love our outhouse. They weren't very noticeable during the day, but they sure enjoyed hanging around the outhouse at night. My sisters and I never went there alone after dark. We would hold a flashlight and shine it around the interior to locate the spiders. After finding the fattest and creepiest ones, we would blind them with the bright light, making them freeze in place for a minute or two. One of us would hold the flashlight while the other one went, as quick as they could. You didn't have much time before the spider would move again. When it was my turn to hold the light, Rose always felt it necessary to keep repeating, "Don't turn the light off, don't turn the light off." I always threatened to, but never did.

There was one time a creepy spider kept me out of the outhouse during broad daylight. I opened the door to the outhouse and set eyes on the scariest spider I had ever met. He was a menacing looking thing, with long hairy legs and plump round body. He was spinning a web right by the toilet seat and was racing back and forth across it. I had a terrible feeling about this spider. I took a minute to consider my limited options… bushes or the outhouse? It was an easy decision because there was no way I was going anywhere near that freak of a spider. I was off to the bushes.

Making my way through the thick foliage, I found what I assumed was the ideal spot. I dropped my drawers and squatted, but sprang right back up again, letting out a bloodcurdling scream. My bottom was on fire! It felt like a swarm of bees had stung me. What on earth had happened? Upon closer inspection, I discovered the source of my distress. I had squatted in a patch of stinging nettle. I was in agony and wishing I had taken my chances with that horrible spider inside the outhouse.

Spiders frightened me, but grasshoppers did not concern me at all. However, grasshoppers absolutely terrified Rose. She wasn't just a little afraid, she was, turn white, scream, and run like mad scared! There were oodles of grasshoppers in the summer, which made Rose very anxious. I had to carry her piggyback whenever we walked through grass or fields. At the first hint of a grasshopper, she would scream, hop up onto my back, and hold on tight until the coast was clear.

There was a large shed beside the outhouse and I loved to rummage through it. It was loaded to the rafters with cool stuff. A lot of the items must have belonged to my grandfather, because they were ancient, and not the sort of junk most folk had in their sheds. There was an old, well used wooden sickle with a long crescent moon shaped blade on it. I tried it out a few times, swinging it back and forth, trying to cut the tall grass, but could not get the hang. There was also a large, scary looking leg-hold animal trap hanging on the wall which I called the bear trap. I would struggle to pry it open, having to use all of my strength. With the trap set, I would poke it with a stick, and it would snap shut, cutting the branch in half. It made me jump every time. There were also some ancient wooden badminton rackets strung with original catgut, and several badminton birdies made of actual bird feathers. We would play badminton over the clothesline with those for hours. Some old heavy wooden darts were also fun to play with. They were about six inches long, with a fat smooth wooden body, and real bird feathers on the ends. The needle was sharp and long. You could throw those darts a mile. I would try to hit the shed, a tree or the outhouse; sometimes reaching my target and occasionally hitting things I hadn't planned on.

A large birdhouse sat on top of the shed. This was not your everyday birdhouse, it was more like a bird mansion. It was very upscale. There were several holes and little doors, each with its own small perch. The roof had tiny wooden shingles, and the siding was a lovely rose color. Swallows claimed that house every year. It was fun to watch them fly in and out of the holes and hang out in our yard. The swallows behaved themselves until their eggs hatched. When the baby birds arrived, the adult birds became attack birds! They would swoop down, coming so close to your head you could feel the breeze from their wings. They changed from friendly to ferocious on the day the babies arrived, and would not stop dive-bombing until you were well away from their house. Trips to the outhouse got interesting during the baby bird stage...

Gabe the Fisherman and a Little Green Rowboat

Lake Winnipeg is the tenth largest fresh-water lake in the world and the sixth largest lake in Canada. I loved taking the old green rowboat out on the lake and stayed out there for hours. I often spotted Gabe the fisherman far out on the lake pulling in his nets. Gabe lived at the lake year-round and sold fish for a living. Battered pickerel was one of my favorite meals, and Gabe sold the best pickerel ever. Gabe was a seasoned fisherman with an old and weathered face. His brother had also been a fisherman, but died after being hit by lightning while hauling in his nets on Lake Winnipeg. Gabe too had been struck by lightning while out on the lake, but unlike his brother, lived to tell about it. The most fascinating thing about Gabe was that he and his wife both had a wooden leg. They both hobbled when they walked. I don't actually know how they lost their legs, but I heard many interesting stories about it through the years.

One day I spotted Gabe way out on the lake. His big boat was just a small dot. I thought it might be fun to row out and see what he was up to. Rose was my passenger, so I shared my idea with her. She did not like the idea at all and questioned the wisdom of going so far out on the lake. Rose was never one to seek thrilling activities, always choosing safe ventures over risky endeavors. I could usually convince her to go along with my plans, even when she resisted. I was the one rowing, so she had no choice but to come along for the ride. I pointed the rowboat towards our target and rowed. Gabe was much further out than he appeared to be when we had spotted him from the shore. The water was getting choppy, and it seemed to take forever to get there. Was Gabe moving further out on the lake, or had I misjudged the distance? The shoreline was now a blur. I kept my eyes on Gabe's boat and continued to row. We were bound to reach it sooner or later.

After much rowing, we finally made it to the grey wooden fishing boat and pulled up alongside. When Gabe saw it was two little girls out on the middle of the lake he hollered, "What do you think you are doing out here?" I shouted back, "We came to see what you are doing!" He seemed concerned but also amused. "I am doing my job, which is fishing." Gabe would string huge nets, held up by little wooden buoys, across the water early in the morning and then pull up the same nets later in the day. He went on working while he talked to us, pulling in his net loaded with fish, throwing some into his boat and others back into the water. He would gut fish and throw the slimy insides into the lake which attracted a massive flock of seagulls. He cut the heart out of one of the larger fish and threw it onto the seat of our rowboat. The heart was still beating and continued to do so for quite a while. It was gross, but also rather interesting.

Gabe had work to do and stopped talking to us. We sat and watched for a while, but the novelty wore off. We shouted goodbye to Gabe, and I pointed our little green rowboat towards the shore. We finally reached land, but it was an awful long way for one small girl to row. It was worth it though. How many little kids get to watch an actual fisherman pull in nets full of fish, or see a real live fish's heart beating right before their eyes? That was so cool…

The Clubhouse on Tenth Avenue

There was a clubhouse down the lane from our cottage. It was a big wooden building with a small canteen that sold milk, bread, pop, ice cream, sunflower seeds, chips, and chocolate bars. Mrs. Partridge ran the canteen and had been there for years. She knew every family that had cabins at Sandy Hook. Us kids never had much money to buy things from her, but bought several five-cent bags of sunflower seeds. Sunflower seeds were something we only ate at the lake. It was okay to throw the shells on the ground when you were at the lake, but unacceptable back home in the city.

A jukebox sat in the corner of the clubhouse. It cost ten cents to play a record. Sometimes a group of us kids would put our money together and agree on a song to play on the jukebox. That took a while because we could never settle on which song to play. Once decided, we would drop the money in, push the correct letters and numbers, and the song would play. When the song was close to the end, someone would bump the jukebox, causing the needle to jump back over the record and start again at the beginning. We would do this over and over until Mrs. Partridge yelled, "Stop whatever it is you are doing, and go outside"!

A movie was played in the clubhouse every Friday evening. The movie was always a highlight of our week. They set up a hundred chairs and charged fifteen cents admission. Mom gave us twenty-five cents each, which meant we had ten cents to spend on pop, a chocolate bar or popcorn. A big screen was lowered from the ceiling and a huge reel of film was set onto the big projector. The film always broke once or twice during the movie and the man operating the projector would scramble to splice the film back together. Every kid in the place stomped their feet on the old wooden floor creating a thundering noise until it was working again. The man struggling to fix the film would always smile and shake his head.

There was an unusual feature involving the clubhouse, and it pertained to the toilet facilities. Two separate outhouses sat on the field outside the clubhouse. One was for the boys and one was for the girls. These were each three-seater outhouses… one wide open room and three holes. This was something you didn't see every day, and it always struck us as odd…

Winnipeg Beach Fun

Winnipeg Beach was three miles from Sandy Hook. It was popular for its amusement park and roller-skating rink. Mom would not allow us to go to the roller rink because she said the "bad kids" hung out there. We loved the amusement park with its penny arcades, shooting gallery, rides, games, and giant wooden roller coaster. A wooden boardwalk ran from one end of the park to the other.

You needed tickets to go on the rides and play the arcade games. My favorite game was the one where you rolled a ball, trying to get it into one of three holes. You would receive yellow tickets as a prize each time you played. The higher your score, the more yellow tickets you would win. We collected these and traded them in at the end of the summer. We had a glass jar in the cottage that held our stockpile of tickets. Dad would let us choose what to purchase and we always had a hard time making our choice. A few of the items we chose over the years were, a cupie doll, a glass flamingo ornament, and a painted glass ashtray. These treasures found a place in our cottage for years to come.

Another of my favorite games was the shooting gallery where you shot a rifle at a bear. The bear had red lights all over his body. When you shot the right spot, the red light would flash, and the bear would rear up, and roar. The quicker you fired, the more often the bear stood up and roared. I would carefully aim the rifle each time I shot, and could hit the bear every single time… at least that's what I thought. I was boasting to Rose about my excellent shooting skills, when a kid overheard and said, "The lights come on and the bear roars every time someone pulls the trigger, if you hit it or not". Well, I sure didn't enjoy being duped like that, and would not be playing that dumb bear game ever again.

My favorite ride was the merry-go-round. I always chose the same black horse because of the way he looked. With his head held high, glowing eyes and flowing mane, it appeared he was racing so fast nobody would be able to catch him. When I sat on that black horse, he came alive in my mind. No one in the world was fast enough to catch us. I also rode the live ponies at Winnipeg Beach, but did not much care for it. For one ticket, you could travel one lap around a well-worn muddy path. I liked the pony, but did not enjoy being walked at a snail's pace by the person holding the rope. I wanted to ride him by myself, and I wanted to gallop. My merry-go-round horse was more fun than the live pony.

I also loved the bumper cars and the boat ride. My favorite boat was the bright red one, and I loved ringing the bell. The tilt-a-whirl was fun, but if you went on more than twice, you would throw up. The old wooden roller coaster was the tallest in all of Canada. It was huge, fast and terrifying. It rattled, creaked and shook, as you inched your way up the track to the top, where you would hover for just a second, before dropping at lightning speed! It scared me to death, and I loved it.

The many games of chance were fun to play. I liked the game where you picked a yellow duck out of the water as they floated past. All I had to do was pick the right duck. Every time I pulled a yellow duck out of the water I was sure that today would be the day, and the huge stuffed animal, expensive looking lamp, or clock radio, would be mine. I carefully studied the parade of yellow ducks as they floated past, putting much thought into my choice. Those ducks disappointed every single time! All I ever won was a cheap pen that didn't even work. I never actually saw anyone win a prize in all the years I went there. That was probably why a thick layer of dust covered the lamps, clock radios, and stuffed animals lined up across the back wall.

Winnipeg Beach had the best candy apples, cotton candy, and rainbow ice cream in the world. At the end of a fun day, dad would let us choose one treat from the concession stand. I always chose a red candy apple or a rainbow ice cream cone. They were both delicious and it was difficult to choose…

Elementary School

I attended Wolseley School from kindergarten to grade six. Wolseley School was a one story, red brick building, one street over from Newman Street. Life turned a little problematic for me once school started. School had a lot of important rules, and there were major consequences when one of those rules got broken. It's not that I didn't understand the concept of rules, or that I was trying to misbehave... things just seemed to happen. Trouble found me when I was not even looking for it. I realized soon into my school career I could not, and should not, do the things that came naturally. I needed to make readjustments to fit in and stay out of trouble. It was possible, but it would not be easy. Teachers often asked, "Why can't you be more like your sister?" or "Why can't you be more like your friend Valerie?" or "Why on earth do you do the things you do?" I never once heard them say, "Good job you're doing being you." I learned that teachers were nothing like my mother. Mom objected to much of what I did and tried her very best to steer me in the right direction, all the while loving me and making me feel valued as a person. My elementary school teachers did not know what to make of me. They struggled to fit this square peg into that round hole most of their students fit so easily into.

I thought kindergarten was fun. There were a lot of great toys, and we played cool games. We played a game called Billy Goat Gruff, where we all took turns being the troll under the bridge, and Squirrel, Squirrel, Who's Got the Nut? I liked story hour, art time and playtime, but loathed naptime. We each had our own little mat which was placed on the floor. We were to lie down, close our eyes and pretend to snooze. Miss Vincent would turn off the lights, lower the blinds, and hum a quiet song. I was not tired, and I did not enjoy lying still, so this was difficult for me.

There was no gum chewing allowed in kindergarten. I did not have access to gum during school hours so I was certain this would not be an issue. I did however get in trouble because of that very rule. I was sitting quietly, listening to a story Miss Vincent was reading, while nibbling at a band-aid on my finger. The band-aid came off, so I kept it in my mouth and chewed on it. Miss Vincent lifted her eyes from the book and scowled. Her sweet, storytelling voice, turned to a scary voice, "Maureen, are you chewing gum?" I had to choose quickly. Should I tell her about the band-aid, or let her think it was gum I was chewing? There was no rule about chewing band-aids in school, but I felt a little embarrassed. I was five years old and perhaps too old for such behavior. Miss Vincent waited for my reply as the whole class looked on. My heart was pounding, and I longed for more time to weigh my options. I ended up making the wrong decision. I chose the lie over the truth and said I was chewing gum. Well, you would think I had just confessed to murdering a little kid on the way to school. She was livid! She set the storybook down, got up from her chair, gripped my little hand, and instructed me to drop my gum, (band-aid) in the wastepaper basket. Apparently, we were making a trip to the principal's office. I didn't know what a principal was, but it didn't sound good. I appeared to be in a great deal of trouble. We marched down the hall and into an office. Miss Vincent spoke to a lady at the front desk but I could not hear what she said. The lady said the principal was in her office, and not too busy to see me. Miss Vincent returned to the safety of the kindergarten classroom, leaving me behind trembling. I wished I was going with her. The principal was a grey haired, scary looking woman. She asked if I had been chewing gum? I knew my lie about the gum had been a mistake. I should have told the truth about the band-aid no matter how awkward it was. Because I didn't want to get into double trouble for lying, I stuck with my original version of the story. The principal lady came close to my face. She asked if I knew we were not allowed to chew gum in school? I responded yes. She asked why I was chewing gum if I knew it was forbidden? I did not have a good answer for that one so kept silent. She warned me not to chew gum in school ever again. I assured her I would never, as long as I lived, chew gum in school. She freed me with a scowl, certain I had learned my lesson. This was the first of many lessons I would learn during my elementary school years at Wolseley School.

I made it through kindergarten and landed in grade one. This was a huge eye opener for me. In grade one they have rows of desks and they expect you to sit in one most of the day. Who comes up with these crazy ideas? On the first day of grade one the teacher provided each of us with a piece of paper to draw on. I was uncertain about what she expected me to draw on the paper because I did not hear the instructions. My ears worked okay, so it is possible I had not been listening. I did not know what to do with this piece of paper. I got bored sitting and staring at it, so got up for a little walk. I walked up one row of desks and down the next. I didn't just walk; I did a walk-hop kind of step. Mrs. Huber stopped me and asked if I had finished my work. I said no, and judging by her reaction, it was not the answer she had been hoping for. Apparently in grade one we do not get up and walk around until we are finished our work. We also listen carefully to instructions and complete what they have told us to do. These were just two of the many important things I learned on my first day of grade one. I learned so many new things, my head was about to burst. There was no way I could remember all of those rules...

The Girl Must Need Glasses

My grade one teacher suggested I might need eye glasses. I was not reading as well as some in my class and she felt the reason might be my eyesight. Mom made an appointment to have my eyes tested. The eye doctors' office was downtown, so we rode the streetcar. We showed up at the scheduled time and were instructed to go straight into the examining room. The doctor had me stand in front of an alphabet chart, and after covering one eye with a little metal paddle, asked me to recite the letters he pointed at. I was in grade one and should have known my whole alphabet, but I occasionally got one or two of my letters mixed up. I hesitated to say them out loud in case I got one wrong. I was only a few feet from the eye chart and could see them all perfectly well, but as I was unsure about one or two and said I couldn't see them. He went to a filing cabinet and flipped through some sheets of paper. He pulled one out and said, "You are in grade two, right?" Because I was uneasy about the eye chart and worried about what he would make me do next, I remained silent and didn't correct him. He must have taken my silence as affirmation because he handed me the typed sheet and asked me to read the story out loud. This grade two story had words in it I had never seen before and it was a lot harder than the stories we read in grade one. I wanted to inform him I was in grade one and not grade two, but I was too nervous to say anything. He kept instructing me to read;

but I didn't want to try. I was afraid of getting it wrong, so told him I couldn't see it. He took a funny looking little light from his pocket, came close to my face, and looked in my eyes. I feared he was checking to see if there was a brain back there. He then placed funny little glasses over my eyes and kept flipping the glass lenses. When he finished checking me out, he wrote something on a piece of paper and went to talk to my mom. He told mom that his examination had confirmed I needed a weak strength of eyeglasses. He showed us several samples and left us to make our decision. It was another week before the glasses were ready. The first day I wore my new glasses to school, my teacher moved me from the back of the classroom to the front row. Now that my desk was front and center, and right under the teachers' nose, I had no choice but to listen and pay attention. It was not long before I was reading perfectly and able to recite the alphabet backwards and forwards with no mess-ups.

I only wore the glasses for one year, because at my next eye appointment I read every letter on the eye chart with no problems. The doctor told mom the glasses had corrected my vision. I suspected that moving my desk from the back of the room to the front, under the watchful eye of the teacher, might have had more to do with remedying my problem than those glasses ever did...

The Dreaded Capital Letter "R"

Things were humming along at school and I had moved up to grade two. My reading was now up to par, and my printing was apparently coming along nicely. I knew I was a satisfactory printer by the end of grade one because my teacher had stopped correcting and criticizing every jot and tittle I dared put to paper. She was a good teacher, but never once told me anything I did was acceptable. This made me question everything I did. It would have been prudent of her to tell me what I had done right occasionally. I would have tried to repeat those things. I guess she didn't think of that.

Miss Shepard was my grade two teacher. I had learned about the Good Shepard in Sunday school, and she was not anything like that one. Miss Shepard was a no-nonsense kind of person, who was going to make me learn no matter what. In grade two we were learning cursive writing. We had gone through the alphabet one letter at a time, working our way up to the capital letter R. We practiced it on paper, over and over, until we got it right. I do not know what my problem with the capital R was, but I could not get my hand to make all the required twists and loops that went into it. No matter how many times Miss Shepard showed me, I still could not do it. She thought it might be a good idea to make me go up to the blackboard in front of the entire class and try to write it there. She wrote a beautiful capital R on the board and told me to copy what she had done. I gave it my best try, but my R did not look much like the one she had written. She repeated this exercise a few times with little success on my part. I am not sure why, but my inability to write a capital R, made her furious! It did not seem to matter to her that I was trying as hard as I could. I did not enjoy being up at the board at the best of times, and the fact I was failing so miserably at this task made it almost unbearable for me. If I could have talked my hand into writing that capital R, believe me I would have. Miss Shepard got frustrated at my lack of success and grabbed me by the shoulders, shaking me back and forth until my teeth rattled. She looked crazed as she shouted at me, "Try harder!" She obviously did not know what a person looked like when they were trying as hard as they possibly could. To my relief, she gave up and sent me back to my desk. She seemed to have concluded that I would never, as long as I lived, be capable of writing that capital letter R. It would appear my fate was sealed. I would live the rest of my life unable to write any words that included the dreaded capital letter R...

Woodpeckers and Blue Jays

Elementary teachers loved to divide their classes into three groups. The three divisions had names such as, Butterflies, Woodpeckers and Blue Jays, or Pansies, Buttercups and Hollyhocks or Oaks, Elms and Evergreens. These groupings showed how proficient you were at reading and writing. Teachers thought they were being discreet using this method, but they weren't fooling anyone. Everyone knew which groups had the best readers and writers, and which groups did not measure up. I always got placed in the middle group. I wasn't the best, and I wasn't the worst.

I was in grade four when my teacher, Miss Rutherford, asked me to stay back for a few minutes at recess. I was eager to get out and play, but you do not say no when your teacher asks you to stay behind. My classmates filed past me and out the door, leaving me alone with Miss Rutherford. I was a little apprehensive and my mind was reeling. I could not, for the life of me, think of anything I had done wrong. There had to be something, but I could not recall a single thing. I waited anxiously for her to speak. Miss Rutherford informed me that my schoolwork of late had been excellent, and she wanted to move me up to the Blue Jays. Well, this was a pleasant surprise. I had never been in the very best group before. I told her I would love to be a Blue Jay.

She helped me move my desk over to the Blue Jay row, and it was settled.

I went out to join the other kids at recess and my friends came rushing over. They were eager to know if I had gotten into trouble. I told them the good news about me being moved up from a Woodpecker to a Blue Jay. My good friend Valarie was genuinely happy for me, but the rest did not seem to care much. It seemed they had hoped for a more exciting story and found this one to be a bit boring...

Grade Six

My least favorite year of elementary school was grade six. The school principal, Miss Read, shared the teaching duties of our class with our homeroom teacher, Miss Compton. I felt very anxious having the principal as a part-time teacher, which made for an uneasy grade six school year. I sometimes got into trouble for things I didn't even do. For instance, the time we were practicing singing for the approaching school concert. Each grade would be singing a song at the concert, and it was our turn to go to the school gym to practice our musical piece. They lined us up on risers in three rows. My spot was in the middle row. Miss Read was the conductor and took her place on a raised box in front of us, as one of the other teachers played the piano. Miss Read's arms swung wildly, causing the loose flab on her upper arms to wave back and forth to the beat of the peppy music. It was comical, but you do not laugh at the school principal and live to tell about it. I didn't want to get into any trouble, so I stayed focused on my singing. I loved to sing, and may have been singing a bit more enthusiastically than the others. My good friend Valerie was in the row in front of me. Valerie was a model student and never got into any trouble. Valarie, for some reason, thought my singing was hilarious. She turned around and burst out laughing. This caused other kids to join in. Miss Read lowered her arms and bellowed, "Enough!" She demanded to know what on earth was going on? Because my best friend Valerie was the one that had turned around and started the laughter, Miss Read asked her what had happened. With no hesitation Valerie snitched, saying, "Maureen was singing loud, and terrible." Miss Read gave me the death stare and ordered me to "Leave!" I left the gym and stood out in the hall awaiting my fate.

Choir practice ended and my classmates paraded past. Most seemed afraid to even look my way for fear they would also get reprimanded. Valerie gave me a brief glance as she passed. Her look suggested she was sorry she had gotten me into trouble. I gave her the stink eye back. Miss Read was the last to exit the gym. She took her place in front of me and scowled. She grabbed my chin between her thumb and index finger and squeezed hard, jerking my chin up and down. I do not recall the exact words she uttered, but I remember staring into her eyes and thinking how unfair it was that she was yelling at me. I had done nothing wrong. I realize I was no angel and my past record was not spotless, but I was innocent this time. I genuinely loved to sing, which is why I was singing with such exuberance. That is why her shouting was not scaring me. She finally stopped yelling and jerking my head up and down and instructed me to go on outside and join the other kids for recess. When I went out the door of the school, Valerie and several others were waiting for me. They were eager to hear what had happened. I felt that a demonstration was better than an explanation. I took Valerie's chin between my thumb and index finger, got close to her face, and shouted the things Miss Read had yelled at me, all the while jerking her head up and down. It was pretty funny, and kids gathered around, laughing and enjoying this re-enactment of events. My comedy act however, came to an abrupt halt when I spotted a face in the window just above our heads. There, taking it all in, stood Miss Read. The crowd scattered and my heart sank. Valarie and I ran to the back of the schoolyard. I had visions of Miss Read tearing out the door and hauling me back into the school to punish me in unimaginable ways. Recess was almost over and I thought for sure my life would also be over once the school bell rang.

The bell rang, and I made my way back to my classroom. I slumped at my desk, fearful of meeting Miss Read. It was however my lucky day, because in walked Miss Compton. By some stroke of good fortune Miss Compton was taking Miss Read's place in our classroom. It still worried me that Miss Read would show up, so I kept my eyes peeled on the door for the rest of the afternoon. When the four o'clock bell rang I was the first one out the door of the school, and I did not stop running until I got to the safety of my home. I strolled into the kitchen where I found mom ironing. She looked up from her stack of ironed laundry and said, "I got a call from Miss Read today." My heart sank as I waited for what was coming next. It turns out Miss Read had phoned mom and told her everything that had taken place at school; including my academy award-winning performance outside her office window. Mom, for some strange reason, was calm. She was using her quiet voice to update me on the details of her discussion with Miss Read. Miss Read told my mother she would make the rest of the school year very hard for me, and had plans to turn my little life around once and for all. She warned mom I would not like her much by the end of grade six, but I would one day thank her for her efforts. Mom assumed Miss Read had things under control and left it in her capable hands.

Grade six was a long, hard year, and I was glad when it finished. Miss Read was harsh and unfair. She had predicted I would not like her much by the end of the year, and she was right. She also claimed I would thank her for her efforts. There are many words I could use to describe how I felt about Miss Read's efforts, and thankful wasn't one. I was relieved when grade six and my elementary school years ended. I was eager to go to a different school for Junior High...

What on Earth?

I attended Isaac Brock School for grades seven to nine and I loved it. I walked to and from school every day with Valerie, chatting the whole way. My new teachers were all nice, and I was doing well in school. There wasn't much to grumble about. Life was good, and I was fitting into an enjoyable routine. However, there was something that occurred right out of the blue and threw me for a loop. I was sitting at my school desk behind Bobby Dolenchuk, the boy with the big brown eyes, dark wavy hair and warm, friendly smile, when I got the oddest feeling in the pit of my stomach. It was as if thousands of butterflies were flapping and fluttering inside me. This odd, yet not an unpleasant sensation, was something I had never experienced before. I was uncertain about what was going on and wondered if Bobby might have something to do with it. He seemed extra nice for a boy, and also very cute. I would definitely discuss this with Valerie on the walk home from school later… she would know.

Valerie didn't laugh when I brought up the topic, but smirked while proclaiming in a bit of a singsong voice, "Maureen has a crush on Bobby Dolenchuk!" Well, perhaps I did. I had been noticing some subtle changes and a lot of them had to do with my attitude towards boys. For the early part of my life I had looked upon all boys as tree climbing companions, bike-riding partners, and equal competitors in all sports and games. I had lost the desire to compete against, outdo, and defeat the male members in my group of friends. I put extra thought into my choice of clothing, and with help from my sister, spent longer than usual getting my hair looking just right.

I looked forward to going to school, and enjoyed sitting behind the boy with the chocolate brown eyes, wavy hair, and warm, friendly smile...

The Teen Years

Elementary school, and those happy-go-lucky tree climbing days were now a faint memory. The fun and transforming years of junior high had finished, and I was off to Gordon Bell for high school.

These years were jam-packed with new adventures, including crushes on boys, community club dances, girls sleepovers, and scores of silly fads and fashions. It was a time of miniskirts, sweat shirts worn inside out, jars of pink Dippity-do hair gel, little blue rubber hair Spoolies, painful prickly hair rollers worn while you slept, record players blasting the songs of The Monkeys', Herman's Hermits, The Lovin' Spoonful, Gerry and the Pacemakers, and Bobby Vinton. When we belted out the love songs, we would insert the name of our latest heartthrob into the lyrics. I continued to enjoy all sports and remained actively involved in basketball, baseball, volleyball, track and field, skating and cross-country. I received the School Athlete Award for Isaac Brock School and for Gordon Bell High School.

I had many interesting summer jobs. I worked in the concession stand at Keystone Dragways, selling dragster burgers while the AA/Fuel dragsters roared down the quarter-mile track. I sold ice cream cones in the pavilion at Assiniboine Park, and I sorted vegetables at Scott National Vegetable Packing Plant with a group of older women who swore like sailors. I put in one summer at Kimberly Clark Paper Plant where I had to open my arms as wide as possible and pick up several boxes of Kleenex off the conveyer belt. I would press hard on each side of the accordion like stack, and struggle not to send the whole works flying across the floor. It took more than a few attempts, and several mishaps, before I finally got the knack.

At sixteen I learned how to drive and loved the independence that came with having a driver's licence. After completing high school I chose to become a Registered Nurse. I started nursing school at the Grace Hospital and lived in the nurses' residence. These years were packed with enough joy, delight, and innocent mischief, to fill countless more pages with silly tales and recollections ... but the telling of those is for another day.

I am in my mid-sixties now and entering a whole new season of life. I honestly do not know where the years have gone. They have slipped by quickly. I've been married for forty-five years, to the wonderful man I met when we were both eighteen years of age. I have raised three incredible children, and I am the proud grandmother of eight absolutely delightful grandchildren. I do not feel old, but when I look in the mirror, I see this older woman looking back at me and it catches me a bit off-guard. Somewhere deep inside, still lives that adventure loving, thrill seeking little girl, and I wonder about that stranger that visits my mirror...

The Stranger in the Mirror

Who is the stranger that visits my mirror?
That older women I see.

She looks a lot like my mother,
But I think that woman is me.

I don't remember that wrinkle,
Or those creases surrounding my lips.

My arms are turning to jello,
And what's going on with those hips?

My hair's never given me trouble,
But it's starting to want its own way.

You'd think it would ask my permission,
Before changing its color to grey.

Those hands are not like my old ones,
They're starting to look a bit worn.

I don't like the brown spots I'm seeing,
And I'm feeling a little forlorn.

Maureen Brooks Slater

The mirror doesn't tell the whole story,
So, I take a step back and reflect

On the life I have lived till this moment;
Could it be that the mirror's incorrect?

Those wrinkles I see on my forehead,
Are from years of care and concern.

It's always best to give it to God,
But it's something we're all slow to learn.

The creases I see when I smile,
Didn't appear overnight.

They're from years of smiling and laughter,
A lifetime of pure delight.

Those arms have cradled a baby.
Those hips held a toddler or two.

My hands could tell a tale of their own,
With all of the things they've been through.

Scrubbing and planting and weeding,
Gently stroking a loved one's head.

Helping and loving and healing,
And putting a child to bed.

The grey in my hair is a visible sign
Of the wisdom I've gleaned through the years.

You *Can't* Climb A Tree In A Dress

All of life's lessons; the good and the bad,
Learned through the laughter and tears.

So, the next time I look in the mirror,
I'll smile at the person I see.

For her and I share a story,
And she'll smile back knowingly.

By,
Maureen Slater

A few more of my poems and thoughts...

(I wrote this for my mother on her 65th Birthday)

When I was just a little girl I used to run and play,
And think up ways to make moms hair,
change from black to grey.

I'd climb the very highest tree straight up to the top.
I loved to hear my frightened mom yell at me to stop!

I used to get quite dirty, I know mom will agree.
Dirt and fun went hand in hand; at least they did for me.

I never caught a lot of fish, but practiced all the time.
It got me into trouble when I downed a power line.

I begged my mom most every day to let me have a pet.
Turtles, hamsters, fish and birds, were all she'd let me get.

A dog was what I wanted; I made it very plain.
And I was so excited, the day that Whiskers came.

Maureen Brooks Slater

I don't know how you managed mom, I kept you on the ball.
The one thing that you must admit, your life was never dull.

And now I have kids of my own, my life is not the same.
Compared to me I must admit, they really are quite tame.

You'll get some satisfaction mom, in what I found today.
I noticed as I combed my hair...I'm starting to go grey!

By,
Maureen Slater

Happy 45th Anniversary Mom and Dad

Forty-five years ago today
You said the words, "I do".
With hopes and dreams you wondered,
What the future held for you.

Times were hard and money scarce,
The depression years were tough.
You didn't live in luxury
But you always had enough.

Your life was blessed with children.
Three girls to love and raise.
You taught them more than you ever knew,
By your kind and unselfish ways.

Your girls are grown women now
With children of their own.
Words aren't enough to thank you,
For the happiness they have known.

Maureen Brooks Slater

You're very special parents,
And although it's seldom said,
Your family loves you very much,
And thank God for the day you were wed.

By,
Maureen Slater

Alzheimer's Can't Steal Our Memories

Alzheimer's crept in slowly and stole our Mom away.
It didn't happen overnight, just little things each day.

"Where did I put my glasses?" and "Have you seen my purse?"
"My memory's not like it was, and it seems it's getting worse."

Our dear and gentle Mother, who made our house a home,
The one who cared for all of us, could no longer live alone.

The one who met life's problems, with such tenacity,
Now felt she was a burden, because of her dependency.

As time progressed the disease did too;
we were running out of hope.
Her confusion and her wandering made it difficult to cope.

Where do you place a Mother that gave everything to you?
We could no longer care for her; "Lord tell us what to do."

And God, who always hears our prayers, extended us His grace,
And opened up a room for Mom, to live at Calvary Place.

Maureen Brooks Slater

The transition wasn't easy, and we shed a tear or two.
But it soon became apparent, it was
the best thing we could do.

The staff were so supportive, and they treated her so well.
The nurses, aides, and cleaning staff, and kitchen personal,

All treated her with dignity, and patience, and respect,
And Pastor Henry saw that all her spiritual needs were met.

Thankyou Lord for Calvary Place, bless all who enter there.
Fill each heart with love and grace, and keep them in your care.

Encourage all the nursing staff, and all the volunteers.
We're grateful for the love they showed
our Mom for all those years.

Yes, Alzheimer's stole Mom's memories,
and caused her to forget.
But our memories have not tarnished,
and we don't live with regret.

We choose to remember the good times,
and all the love she has shown.
To her husband, daughters, grandkids and
friends, and everyone else she has known.

By,
Maureen Slater...Marjorie Brooks' daughter

A Gramma's Heart

I remember it so well. Curtis and Karyn had come over to show us their honeymoon pictures of Italy. When they got to the last picture, there was a "date" written. I didn't understand what they were getting at, and it took a while to figure out it was their way of telling us Karyn was pregnant. We were overjoyed! They were both so excited, and I had never seen Curt so happy. I knew he would be a wonderful dad, and that Karyn would be an awesome mom. We were thrilled at the thought of being grandparents to this new little baby.

It was May 13, 2011 when we got the call from Curtis saying he had taken Karyn to the hospital. The ultrasound Karyn had that day, showed the baby was not growing as it should. Curt told us the Doctor would give Karyn steroids for two days and then do a C-section to deliver the baby. My heart sank as I realized how tiny this baby would be at only 33 weeks along. I told Curtis that his dad and I would pray for all of them... and boy did we pray.

Curt phoned us on May 15, to tell us Karyn had just given birth to a 3 lb. 5 oz. baby boy. He sounded like such a proud dad and I could hardly wait to meet our tiny new grandson, Jake.

Curt called the next day and said the Doctor had ordered genetic testing on Jake because they suspected Down Syndrome. I struggled to be calm and reassuring as I spoke to my son, but inside I was a wreck. I could hear the concern in his voice and I wanted to make it all better. I did the only thing I could think of... I prayed.

Curt called later and told us the test results showed that Jake had Down Syndrome. His voice was strained and I could tell he was having a hard time keeping his composure. My heart broke for my son, my daughter-in-law, and for the unknown future that lay ahead.

Curt's dad and I went to church as usual on Sunday. My heart was so heavy and I had so much that I needed to talk to God about. In the row, directly in front of us, sat a mom, dad, and their two teenage sons. I had never seen this family in church before. It did not take long for me to notice that the one teenage boy had Down Syndrome. I could not take my eyes off of him. I observed this family interact with the boy, and with each other. The service started and the boy with the Down Syndrome kept gently poking his brother trying to get him to look at something he had drawn on a paper. The older brother looked at the drawing and grinned encouragingly before kindly motioning for him to "shh"... The boy with the Down Syndrome smiled and went back to his drawing. A few minutes later he leaned over and whispered something in his brother's ear. The brother listened patiently and chuckled quietly at whatever it was he had said, and once again motioned for him to "shh"... A few minutes passed before the boy with the Down Syndrome thought of something else that just "needed" to be shared with his brother. Again, the brother patiently and lovingly responded to him. The parents at this point both looked over at the boy, smiled kindly, and made

You Can't Climb A Tree In A Dress

a soft "shh" sound to him. The boy with the Down Syndrome grinned, nodded, and rested his head on his brother's shoulder; where it stayed for the rest of the church service.

God used this family to speak comfort, encouragement and hope to my unsettled spirit and hurting heart. It was going to be okay, and the future looked bright.

Jake has been an absolute joy and blessing to our entire family. He is an amazing little guy that has the ability to light up the room. I can say with complete sincerity, Jake is a special gift to our family, and I am so grateful that God trusted us with him.

By,
Maureen Slater

Our Jake

God created everything, the heavens, sky and earth.
And God created babies, and the miracle of birth.

He made those tiny little hands, He made those teeny toes.
He made that little tummy, and that perfect little nose.

He knows each little person before they're even born.
He knit each one together; in the womb, so safe and warm.

He sees each one as perfect, He's familiar with their ways.
He promises to hold them fast, and guide them all their days.

He chose a special family for His precious little Jake.
He knew that he would be so loved,
God's choice was no mistake.

God knew Jakes special challenges, might
cause their hearts to ache,
And seeing them in so much pain, would
make His own heart break.

God gives no explanation, and yet He gives us Hope.
And asks that we would trust in Him, for
the strength in which to cope.

Maureen Brooks Slater

Hope's not about what isn't, I often times forget.
Hope for us is so much more, it's about what isn't yet.

All the days ordained for Jake had long ago been planned.
We hold on to God's promise, that one-day we'll understand.

God loves you so much baby Jake, our family loves you too.
You truly are a gift from God, and we thank the Lord for you.

By,
Maureen Slater (Jakes Gramma)

Proverbs 21:26

("The righteouses give without sparing")

Jesus called me to Himself.
I asked Him to come in.
He shed His blood upon the cross,
To cleanse me of my sin.
Redemption came at such a cost,
He did that just for me.
So I could have new life in Him,
He paid my penalty.
He's blessed my life so richly,
There's nothing that I lack.
Everything I have is His,
I gladly give it back.

By,
Maureen Slater

I Sing Praises To Your Name Lord

I can hear your voice in the thunder,
Your blessings pour down like the rain.
I'm humbled by how much you love me,
How you know me and call me by name.

I can hear your voice in the stillness,
When you whisper and tell me you're there.
When the stress of the day overwhelms me,
I'm comforted knowing you care.

Where can I flee from your presence?
Not the heavens or depths of the sea.
In your presence the night is turned into day.
The darkness can't hide you from me.

Your blessings to me are abundant,
There's nothing on earth that I lack.
My heart overflows and I sing songs of praise,
As my way of loving you back

By,
Maureen Slater

God's Invitation

Come to me all who are burdened,
Heartbroken, weary and stressed.
Find refuge and strength in my presence,
Protection and much needed rest.

I'm gentle and my yoke is easy.
I promise you rest for your soul.
Come under my wing, I will shelter.
Trust me and give me control.

I am your rock and salvation,
Protector, healer, strong tower.
I'm waiting for you, come just as you are.
Have faith in my saving power.

By,
Maureen Slater

All Dogs Go to Heaven

God created everything,
All creatures great and small.
The Bible says He loves each one,
And cares when sparrows fall.

I think when God created dogs,
He did it with a smile.
He knew those little balls of fur
Would really be worthwhile.

Folks would have a faithful friend
To stay close by their side.
A never-ending source of fun,
Devotion, love, and pride.

God made their lifespan very short,
We wouldn't have them long.
And we would grieve and miss them so
Long after they were gone.

Maureen Brooks Slater

Thoughts of them would linger,
And we'd hate to be apart,
But we'd always have fond memories
To carry in our heart.

By,
Maureen Slater

I Was Just Being A Dog (a true story told by my dog Gunner)

You left me home all afternoon, I got a little bored.
I thought I'd check the pantry out, it begged to be explored.

You left the door wide open, and that was very kind.
I therefore went and helped myself, I didn't think you'd mind.

I ate the bags of candy, consumed the peanut mix.
I gobbled up those suckers, and then spit out the sticks.

I finished off the cookies and sampled whole grain rice.
I then enjoyed some honey, with the crackers, it's quite nice.

I gulped it down and swallowed it, extremely fast and quick.
My stomach didn't like it much, I suddenly felt sick.

I needed to be let outside, I ran straight to the door.
I scratched and waited, squirmed a bit, my tummy was so sore.

I stood right there, I didn't move, unsure of what to do.
I needed that door open now, I really had to poo!

You weren't home, I couldn't wait, I had to let it go.
The diarrhea shot right out, I couldn't stop the flow.

Maureen Brooks Slater

And then my stomach started up, it wasn't feeling good.
I threw up all that junk I ate; got rid of all I could.

When you came home and looked around,
you seemed extremely mad.
But I'd forgotten what I'd done; forgot that I'd been bad.

You didn't greet me nicely, or smile and say hello.
You stormed around and shouted, "The
mess", "The smell", "Oh no"!

Who is that dog named Naughty? Whose name I heard you yell.
I was home all by myself, as far as I could tell.

It puzzled me to watch you fume, I could not comprehend.
I did my best to comfort you, because you're my best friend.

I love you more than life itself, I'm loyal, faithful, true.
If you were ever threatened, I'd risk my life for you.

So, when you've done your mopping up, let's go out for a walk.
You seem to be a little stressed, and it always helps to talk.

By,
Maureen Slater

Gunner is Sorry About Your Shoe Mandi

I'm sorry that I chewed your shoe
And spit it on the floor.
My owner said that I was bad,
And that's what bones are for.

I like the toys she bought me,
And I love the rawhide chews.
But nothing really quite compares
To a pair of human shoes.

I like the smell, I like the taste,
I like the way they feel.
I like the way the leather rips,
It makes a tasty meal.

I'm still a little puppy,
I'm not yet very old.
And I could use a lot more work,
On doing what I'm told.

Maureen Brooks Slater

Until I can be trusted,
You could really help me out,
By hiding all your footwear,
Whenever I'm about.

I hope that I'm forgiven,
Cause I think you're really nice.
And I will try as best I can,
Not to do it twice!

By,
Maureen Slater

Heaven Has a Dog Park

When you love a little puppy
You give away your heart.
Puppies know when they are loved
Because they are quite smart.

We cuddle them, and spoil them,
And make a lot of fuss.
It's really not about the dog,
It's what they do for us.

Dogs are always faithful,
Loyal, staunch and true.
God made them for a purpose,
He knew what they would do.

He smiles when He sees the bond
Between a dog and man.
It comes as no surprise to Him,
It's part of His great plan.

It breaks God's heart to call them home,
He knows that we'll be sad.
He promises to care for them,
For that we should be glad.

Maureen Brooks Slater

When we reach Gods' Heaven,
We'll see our pups once more.
The reunion will be awesome,
When they bolt through Heaven's door!

By,
Maureen Slater

(Written on the passing of Junior)

(The poem I read at Shannon's bridal shower)

Our baby girl was finally here; we welcomed her with pride.
She looked so small in her daddy's
arms as he carried her inside.

Her brother ran to meet us, he had waited for this day.
But she was only little, not yet big enough to play.

We marvelled at her cleverness so unashamedly.
This child was something special, surely
all the world could see.

She learned to sit; she learned to crawl,
and then she learned to talk.
At an early age she learned to run; she never seemed to walk.

She loved her dolls and dress-up clothes
and played for hours on end.
Sometimes dressing up the dog, if she couldn't find a friend.

"Can I have a hamster? Can I have a cat?
A guinea pig, fish, cockatoo?"
"And mom we need a second dog; I know you want one too."

Maureen Brooks Slater

Drama was a special love; the stage was what she chose.
We won't forget that final act, and the
punch that broke her nose.

Gymnastics, figure skating, dance, were things she loved to do.
And she excelled at all of these; ringette and soccer too.

Shannon is a runner and had great success at track.
Most of her opponents only got to see her back.

It was bound to happen, and it came as no surprise.
The day we heard the reason for the sparkle in her eyes.

"Mom, I met the cutest boy, I met him at the dance."
"He's tall, good-looking, kind and nice;
I might give him a chance."

The first date proved it isn't dead that thing called chivalry.
For he arrived with flowers, some for
Shannon and some for me.

You couldn't help but like him, I really was quite moved.
I knew this boy was special... because
even her father approved!

By,
Maureen Slater

I Am Sitting Under the Tuscan Sun

I am in Tuscany, Italy. Our room for the week is in an old castle at the top of a hill. Our hotel, Castel Bigozzi, is one of the oldest castles in this area. The grounds surrounding the hotel are stunning and allow for remarkable views of the Tuscan countryside.

I sit in a comfortable chair, on the peak of the hill. It's an ideal spot to read, and I am eager to get back to my book, but my mind wanders. I am aware of the sounds that break through the silence. I hear a chorus of birds; whistling, singing, tweeting. It's more than just a sound, it's music.... a symphony perhaps. This blended bird song is bursting with life and stirs a place deep within my soul. Never in my life, have I experienced such keen awareness of my surroundings.

I am here to relax and catch up on my reading. I seek stillness and calm from the hectic pace I left back home. Again, I am drawn away from my book. Far off in the distance I hear the distinct call of a Coo Coo bird, "Coo Coo, Coo Coo, Coo Coo". That soft and pleasant song stands out from the rest. It's a friendly sound.... nothing like the annoying Coo Coo clock back home that pressures me to get busy. This sound is quiet and calming.

Maureen Brooks Slater

I put my book aside and take time to enjoy the breathtaking sights and sounds. I wish I were an artist, able to paint a portrait of all I see. To the south are beautiful green trees that seem to go on forever. To the east is a magnificent vineyard. The deep-rooted young grapevines look like rows of soldiers, lined up in perfect formation. Heavy clusters of grapes hang from the vines; thankful for yesterday's life-giving rain and the hot Tuscan sun today. To the west, as far as the eye can see, are beautiful green, rolling hills. Describing them as green doesn't do them justice. The hills are a remarkable mixture of every possible shade and hue of the color green. God's paint palate is so much richer than anything man could ever replicate. The color green is not limited in God's hands.

The hillside is sprinkled with old houses and red terra cotta rooftops, which add a delightful contrast to the beautiful landscape. The Cypress trees stand tall and majestic, like Tuscan sentinels. They embody the very essence of Tuscany and create the unique Tuscan backdrop.

I feel content and blessed to be here. I am keenly aware of God's presence and so thankful for this special time alone with Him.

"I needed the quiet…. and He drew me aside"

Maureen Slater

A Norman Rockwell painting done in 1927, of an old man standing on a hilltop, his arm around a young boy, a dog at his side, inspired this poem. They are gazing out to sea at the ships in the distance, and I wondered what the old gentleman might be telling the boy. This is what I imagined...

Old Man Gazing Longingly Out to Sea

Oh, the adventures I've been on.
I've sailed to lands unknown.
Aboard majestic sailing ships,
Across the seas I've flown.

I've been on ships with masts so tall
They almost reach the sky.
White sails flap then catch the wind,
Across the waves I'd fly.

I've hauled in ropes with calloused hands,
Swabbed worn old decks with pleasure.
I've battled storms and choppy seas,
Fought pirates for their treasure.

I've been around this world and back.
Seen things you'll not believe.
And you can travel with me lad,
Through tales that I will weave.

I wouldn't trade this life of mine,
I could not wish for more.
My imagination lets me roam...
Though I've never left this shore.

By,
Maureen Slater

I'm Old Enough to Just Be Me

I don't think of myself as old, until I glance in mirrors.
Inside I'm pretty much the same; it doesn't change with years.

My body's changed, of that I'm sure; I feel new aches and pain.
My hair has turned much greyer, and my skin is not the same.

I've wrinkles, bags and brownish spots and extra skin galore.
My body parts seem in a race, to be first to the floor!

Often times I close my eyes, and ponder what's inside,
The place the younger me and child, still happily reside.

The older me is kinder; forgives mistakes I've made.
If God forgives me, so should I; my debts have all been paid.

I'm caring less what people think, content to be myself.
All those self-improvement books can stay right on the shelf!

The folks that really matter, accept me as I am.
I like the person I've become; my life is not a sham.

I'm not in competition, and life is not a race.
I'm thankful God is patient and extended me His grace.

Maureen Brooks Slater

I'm wiser now and spend my time, with
things that bring me pleasure,
Grandkids, family, time with friends, the things I truly treasure.

Age has its advantages, it's somehow set me free,
To be the person that I am, and permission to be me.

By,
Maureen Slater

Made in the USA
Middletown, DE
15 September 2019